This book is dedicated to the children
at Great Ormond Street Hospital
and everyone who cares for them

THE
ASKITALIAN
Cookbook

EASY-TO-PREPARE RECIPES FROM
THE ASK ITALIAN KITCHENS

edited by **CARLA CAPALBO** with special recipes by **THEO RANDALL** and other expert friends

photography by Jamie Laing, Sylvie Tata and Carla Capalbo

VIKING
an imprint of
PENGUIN BOOKS

CONTENTS

1   ANTIPASTI: STARTERS

2   PRIMI: PASTA

3 PRIMI: RISOTTO, FARRO AND POTATOES

4 PIZZA

5   SECONDI: FISH AND MEAT

BRANZINO CON VERMOUTH E LIMONE Sea bass in lemon, basil and vermouth sauce 127
CALAMARI RIPIENI Stuffed calamari 129
POLLO CON PROSCIUTTO E MASCARPONE Chicken with mascarpone and prosciutto 133
TAGLIATA DI MANZO Sliced steak with rocket and tomatoes 134
SALTIMBOCCA Beef rolls with sage and ham 135
MAIALE AL FORNO Pork loin wrapped in coppa di Parma 136
PATATE E FINOCCHI GRATINATI Potato, fennel and Parmesan gratin 137
SPALLA D'AGNELLO CON OLIVE Slow-cooked lamb shoulder with anchovies, olives and rosemary 139

6   CONTORNI: SALADS AND VEGETABLES

INSALATA CAPRESE Tomato, mozzarella and basil salad 143
INSALATA DI RUCOLA Rocket salad 143
INSALATA DI FORMAGGIO DI CAPRA Goat's cheese salad 144
TONNO E FAGIOLI Tuna and bean salad 146
INSALATA DI SALMONE Smoked salmon salad 147
INSALATA DI POLLO E PANCETTA Chicken salad with pancetta 149
Honey and mustard dressing 149
Chef's salad 150
Chicken Caesar salad 151
VERDURE AL FORNO Roasted mixed vegetables 152
PISELLI CON PANCETTA Peas with pancetta 153
PEPERONATA Stewed peppers 154
FAGIOLINI VERDI CON POMODORO Green beans with tomatoes 154

7   DOLCI: DESSERTS

TORTA MORBIDA DI CIOCCOLATO Soft chocolate cake 158
CREMA DI MASCARPONE Mascarpone cream 158

8 SAUCES AND BASICS

AN INTRODUCTION FROM

HARVEY SMYTH
ASK Italian

A couple of years ago we set out on an exciting new journey: to build ASK Italian into a family of really special restaurants based on a single source of inspiration – our love of Italian food and the Italian culture of cooking and eating. This has inspired everything we do, from sourcing our ingredients, preparing our recipes and training our chefs to our fresh, bold Milanese-influenced design. We're all focused on even the smallest details to make everything perfect every time.

This is a journey of discovery for everyone at ASK Italian, and one that has inspired a number of friends to join us. Real experts like Theo Randall, Carla Capalbo and Adrian Garforth MW, as well as some great Italian friends like the Greci brothers, who make our passata di pomodoro, and the Esposito brothers, who produce our extra virgin olive oil in Puglia. Each member of our team is involved with tastings and trips that explore Italian culture and food. Increasingly, our customers have started to join them on that journey.

Our cookbook contains delicious, easy-to-make recipes from our kitchens, our expert friends and our team members. It's our way of sharing some of the great Italian dishes we've discovered.

It's also a way to help to raise money for our favourite charity. We've worked with Great Ormond Street Hospital Children's Charity for a number of years now. It is a charity we feel really passionate about and which our teams love supporting. We recently raised funds to build a ward kitchen and an adolescent recreation and dining room in the hospital's new Cardiac ward. Our new goal is to raise a further £1 million over the next few years to fund recreational facilities in the new Surgery Centre, which will help provide physical and emotional support to patients and their families.

A minimum of £1 from every cookbook sold will go directly to Great Ormond Street Hospital Children's Charity, making a real difference to the lives of the hospital's patients and their families.

We hope you will enjoy cooking the dishes in the book and, more importantly, enjoy eating them with your family and friends.

Thank you for your support.

Harvey

Harvey Smyth, ASK Italian

TIM JOHNSON
Great Ormond Street Hospital Children's Charity

Great Ormond Street Hospital treats some of the most seriously ill children from all over the UK. Many of these patients have complex and unique conditions that require expertise only the hospital can provide and their doctors and nurses are amongst the very best in the world. Unfortunately not all of the clinical buildings mirror these high standards. This is why Great Ormond Street Hospital Children's Charity is currently fundraising to rebuild two thirds of the hospital, enabling it to help more children and making cramped and outdated wards a thing of the past.

We would not be able to turn this vision into a reality without the wonderful support we receive from companies such as ASK Italian Restaurants, who have created this lovely recipe book for us.

This is part of an extremely generous commitment made by ASK Italian Restaurants to raise £1 million over the next three years. These funds will make a real difference to the lives of patients and their families by funding the dining rooms, play areas and kitchen within the hospital's new Surgery Centre, due to open in 2016. These modern facilities will provide space in which to eat, play and relax: a space designed to be as normal as possible, during what can be a stressful and traumatic time.

By buying the ASK Italian Cookbook you are helping Great Ormond Street Hospital to look after the thousands of sick children that go through its doors each year. On behalf of the patients, families and staff, thank you.

Tim Johnson

Executive Director

Great Ormond Street Hospital Children's Charity

To find out more about the amazing work taking place at Great Ormond Street Hospital, visit www.gosh.org

Children at Great Ormond Street Hospital taking part in a painting project to be used to decorate the Southampton Row ASK Italian restaurant

THEO RANDALL
ASK Italian Expert Friend

My love of everything Italian started at a very early age. I have fond memories of trips to Italy on family holidays. The food we ate was very simple but made a lasting impression on me.

When I think back to my childhood, it's not surprising I became a chef because, for me, good food was very much part of growing up. My strongest memories are of being around a dinner table, at a picnic or even in a remote restaurant on holiday. This made me realize how important family meals are, as they bring everyone together in one place to communicate and enjoy good food.

Great Ormond Street Hospital is such a much-loved institution, helping an amazing number of children every year, and I feel very proud to be part of this book.

I have been working with ASK Italian not only to improve the quality of their food but also to inspire the team. The restaurants have had a lot of time and energy spent on them, as you will see when you visit them. The menus have been written with one idea in mind: to produce fresh, consistent Italian food that is simple but delicious. With every season there are Specials that celebrate the time of year.

The recipes I have contributed are what food should be: simple, delicious and not over-complicated. Having spent many years as Head Chef of the River Café and now with my own London restaurant – Theo Randall at the InterContinental – Italian food is what I love. It has such diversity because each region has its own identity. I still get inspired on every trip to Italy, whether it's by an ingredient, a dish, a place or a person. They're at the heart of my favourite memories.

I hope this book will inspire you to cook, as cooking is simple: all you need is confidence and good taste.

Theo Randall

Chef Theo Randall with ASK Italian team members

CARLA CAPALBO
ASK Italian Expert Friend

Italian food is the most popular in the world. It's loved for its pure, simple flavours, colourful recipes and informal dishes. Who wouldn't list pasta and pizza among their favourite foods?

The great thing about Italian food is that it's easy to prepare. It's more about using seasonal foods with lots of flavour than complicated cooking techniques. Italian recipes are simple to follow and can be adapted to whatever is available. Italian food doesn't rely on expensive products for its successes, but can turn a handful of vegetables into a colourful minestrone soup, or a tin of tomatoes and a packet of pasta into a magnificent spaghetti al pomodoro with just a few flavourings.

Italy's 20 regions are each the source of different cuisines, from northern Piedmont and Emilia Romagna, with their love of egg-rich, hand-made noodles, to the southern regions of Campania and Sicily where olive oil reigns over superb vegetables and fish.

We've gathered a great selection of Italian recipes from north and south into this book. Many come from ASK Italian's menus, with additions from Theo Randall, some of our Italian friends and from me. We hope you'll enjoy them as much as we do by cooking and serving them at home with your families and children.

Great Ormond Street Hospital has been an inspiration to us all during the making of this book. My visits there have confirmed that family love is the most important gift we have, and cooking good food to share with our families is always at the heart of our lives.

My work with ASK Italian has been to share my knowledge about Italian gastronomy — I've been living in Italy and writing about Italian food and wine for over 20 years — and to help the lovely people working in the restaurants become inspired by the character and quality of Italian food culture. Whether it's by taking trips to experience authentic Italian meals, or by making pasta by hand with some of the ASK Italian teams, it's been a worthwhile and pleasurable journey. After all, what could be better than to help improve the food we eat with our kids and families, at home or in our favourite neighbourhood restaurants?

Carla Capalbo

THE ITALIAN LARDER

Carla says: The Italian kitchen contains a few basic ingredients that are useful for preparing many of these recipes. They will help you make your Italian food taste and look more authentic.

EXTRA VIRGIN OLIVE OIL

The most important of these, the keystone of all Mediterranean cooking, is good extra virgin olive oil. The olive is a fruit, and the best olive oil is simply the 'juice' of this fruit: oil is made from crushing fresh olives. Extra virgin olive oil is better than plain olive oil because the 'extra virgin' means it has been crushed mechanically as opposed to having been extracted chemically or by heating.

As with wine, there are many small artisan producers who grow their own fruit and make their oil with love and care. Their oils are usually far better than industrial oils, which look like a bargain at the supermarket but have less flavour and may have been made using industrial short cuts. A bottle of fine extra virgin olive oil may feel like an extravagance, but it will more than repay itself by turning good meals into great ones. It will also last much longer than a similarly priced bottle of wine.

ASK Italian's extra virgin olive oil is made the way it should be by a family in Puglia. It's available from all the restaurants.

Olive oil is sensitive to heat and light so store yours in a cool, dry, dark place. Don't store it above the cooker, where it will get too hot. Unlike wine, olive oil doesn't improve with age, so don't buy too much of it at one time.

EQUIPMENT

You don't need any special equipment to cook most of the recipes in this book, though if you want to make home-made pasta you will have to get a hand-cranked pasta machine or a metre-long rolling pin. For boiling pasta, a very large saucepan is best. You will need scales that give their weights in grams, and a set of standard measuring spoons. In this book, 1 tablespoon is 15ml.

PARMESAN AND GRANA PADANO CHEESES

Both of these great cow's milk cheeses come from northern Italy. Parmesan — or Parmigiano Reggiano as it is called in Italy — is the more famous of the two cousins, but both have earned their 'DOP' (protected origin denomination) classification. It's illegal to imitate or copy them, so if you buy them in their original packaging you know you are getting the real thing. The Italians use Parmesan and Grana on everything, from salads to pasta, and these cheeses give an authentic flavour to all Italian food.

TOMATOES

Always look for ripe tomatoes when cooking Italian food. If they are not in season, imported plum tomatoes can be a great alternative as they will have been picked when the tomatoes were at their ripest and sweetest. Passata is just strained tomatoes, and is an easy-to-use ingredient in sauces and soups. Sun-dried tomatoes are much more intense and can add lots of flavour to your dishes. Soak them for a few minutes in warm water before using if you are not going to cook them, as this helps release some of their concentrated sugars.

GARLIC

The Italians use much less garlic than most people think. They often give their dishes a subtle hint of garlic by heating two whole cloves of peeled garlic in the olive oil at the start of a sauce, and removing it once the sauce has cooked, before serving. If you prefer using finely chopped garlic but find that it sometimes burns, try Theo Randall's trick: chop the garlic and mix it into a spoonful of olive oil before adding it to the pan.

CAPERS

The caper is the flower bud of a bush (Capparis spinosa) which grows all around the Mediterranean. These buds have to be picked just after dawn, before the beautiful flowers bloom. In Sicily and southern Italy, where the best capers come from, they are cured in sea salt. You can find salt-cured capers more easily now in the UK, and they give a distinctive accent to any dish. Just rinse a spoonful of the capers in warm water in a bowl for a few minutes before using, as they are intensely salty. Caper berries, the seed pods of the same bush, are also available, in salt or vinegar. Try them as an aperitivo, or as part of a mixed antipasto.

WINE

We've included some great tips about how to pair wine with Italian food, so see pages 22-25.

ABOUT OUR RECIPES

Most of the recipes in this book are from the ASK Italian menus. You'll be able to spot the recipes that have been given to us by our expert friends in the introductions to each recipe. Theo Randall's recipes, for example, start with 'Theo says:' and give his personal introduction to the dish.

ITALIAN WINE

We are delighted to be working with our expert friend, Adrian Garforth MW (Master of Wine), one of only 298 MWs in the world. Adrian has helped select our all-Italian wine list so that you can drink well without breaking the bank when eating in our restaurants. Just like Italy's regional cuisine, its wine reflects the character and flavours of the specific areas in which it is made. Our small but varied wine list showcases this diversity.

Adrian has toured the UK to introduce the new list to our restaurant managers and staff and to help them pair our wines with food. We asked him to give us some tips about wine for the book.

ADRIAN SAYS:

Most Italians would never dream of having a meal without a glass of Italian wine to go with it. Food and wine is such a part of the culture there that they instinctively know what wine they like and how to match it with food. For the rest of us, wine selection is often more of a challenge, particularly as Italian wines may be named after the grape variety (Sangiovese, Pinot Grigio or Fiano) or the region in which they are made (Chianti, Barolo and Soave).

Given this potential for confusion we've found the key to understanding Italian wine is to look at the map. Italy is a long narrow boot that travels through several climate zones, from the cool north to the baking-hot south. The grapes that are used to make wine are a fruit like any other, so their flavours reflect their growing conditions.

In the north, with vineyards in the shadows of the Alps and Dolomites, the cool climate means that fruit does not ripen as fully as further south. The grapes are higher in acidity and relatively low in sugar, producing wines that are lighter, crisp and refreshing in style. As you progress towards the south, passing through the central regions of Tuscany and Umbria, the grapes become progressively riper. By the time you arrive in the 'heel' of Puglia or onto the volcanic island of Sicily, intense sun produces grapes that are brimming with sweetness and full of ripe, tropical flavours. These changes define the different styles of Italian wines and are easy to pick out when you taste them.

If you like white wine that is refreshing and relatively light in flavour, look for northern Italian wines such as Pinot Grigio or Gavi. The wines from the south tend to be more full-bodied and higher in alcohol, with ripe fruit flavours.

If this is more your style, try a luscious native red from Puglia, such as Primitivo. Wines from the central areas such as Chianti combine the best of both worlds.

Wine selection is always a matter of personal preference so don't hesitate to try out the different wines on our list to discover what kinds of Italian wines you like best.

WHICH WINE WITH WHAT FOOD?

When it comes to food, similar principles apply, which explains why local wine is so often the best match for regional food. We're so used to hearing the old rule that 'white wine goes with white meat and red wine with red meat'. But what if you prefer a crisp red Valpolicella with your sole? That's perfectly fine by us. We've created a few guidelines to help you make those choices.

It's more important to pair foods with wines of a similar flavour intensity than to worry too much about their colour. Light food, whether it's a salad or piece of fish, is best matched with a light wine, such as Soave or Valpolicella. More robust dishes, like a rich Bolognese meat sauce, are best enjoyed with full-flavoured wines. Try it with our wonderfully fruity Primitivo or a Nero d'Avola from the south of Italy. This balancing act will help you make the right choices.

TRENTINO

VENETO

FRIULI VENEZIA GIULIA

AOSTA VALLEY

LOMBARDY

PIEDMONT

EMILIA-ROMAGNA

LIGURIA

TUSCANY

UMBRIA

MARCHE

LAZIO

ABRUZZO

MOLISE

CAMPANIA

SARDINIA

BASILICATA

PUGLIA

CALABRIA

SICILY

OUR WINE TASTING GUIDE

Adrian's created a simple six-point guide to help you find the right wine.

SPARKLING – WHITE

It's no surprise to find that sales of Prosecco, the lovely Italian sparkling wine, are on the increase. Prosecco is the perfect way to start an Italian meal, so try some for your next aperitivo.

Wine is really all about enjoyment. The Italians are masters of drinking wine as an accompaniment to their delicious food. Why not join them and explore our Italian wine selection with confidence by following these simple guidelines. If you want more help, don't hesitate to consult our team members at ASK Italian. Saluti!

CRISP AND ELEGANT – WHITE AND RED WINES

The grapes for these wines are usually grown in northern Italy or in mountainside vineyards at higher altitudes, where the long, cool growing season produces wines with refreshing fruit quality and mineral complexity underpinned by lovely acidity.

White examples of this type include our Gavi or Garganega from the Soave region. Or try a red Rosso Veronese from the vineyards in Valpolicella. All these wines match well with delicately flavoured salads and simple pasta dishes.

MEDIUM-BODIED, REFRESHING AND FRUITY – WHITE AND RED WINES

These wines are produced in warmer areas, such as the central regions of Tuscany and Umbria, or in the warmer parts of the Veneto. Whites here are medium-bodied with good fruit concentration, and have a crisp finish.

We're thinking of our Pinot Grigios, or the Verdicchio from the Marche region. Reds of this style are still soft but fruitier, with the flavours of cherry and red berries. The bolder flavours in this group of wines complement pizza or spicy pasta dishes like the arrabbiata.

RIPE AND FRUITY – WHITE, ROSÉ AND RED WINES

Made from grapes ripened under the intense southern sun, these wines show lots of fruit concentration but are still soft and easy to drink. Look no further than to our Puglian pair of white Bianco Salento and juicy red Primitivo, or to our pink Sicilian Rosato. They go really well with the full flavours of dishes such as Bolognese sauce and lasagne.

FULL-BODIED AND COMPLEX – RED WINES

Wines made from ripe grapes that have more structure and body often have more complex flavours as a result of being aged in wooden barrels. Try a Chianti Classico, an Amarone or our mature Nebbiolo from the Barolo area in Piedmont, in north-western Italy. Pair these wines with hearty, meaty dishes that can match their structure and complexity, such as roast lamb shoulder or sliced steak.

SWEET – WHITE

Most of us love sweet things, even if we don't like to admit it. Drinking sweet wines can be an unexpected and enjoyable experience. These wines can only be made from super-ripe grapes that often have traditional methods of production.

It's quite an art to stop a wine from tasting overly sweet or cloying by retaining its natural acidity and fruit flavours. Our Recioto di Soave is a wonderful match with dessert. The lightly sparkling Moscato d'Asti also works well with desserts and is great as an aperitif. Ours has been made by one of Piedmont's top producers.

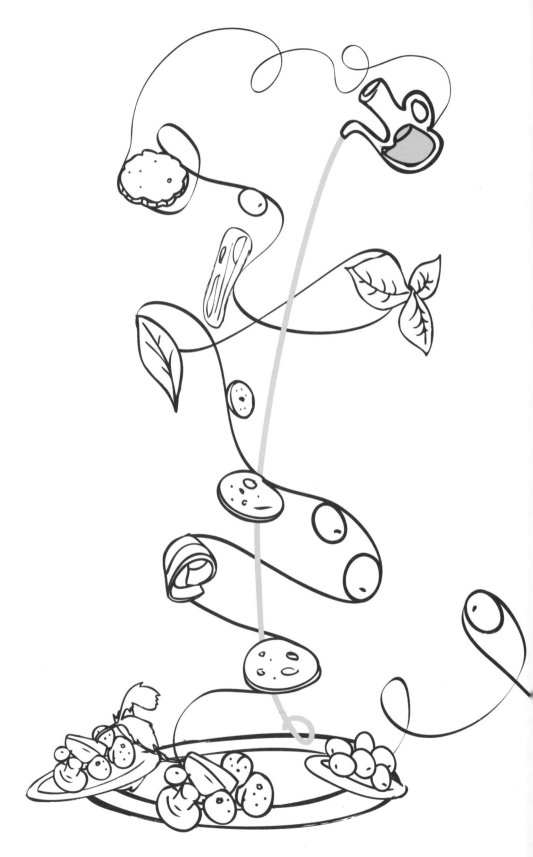

CHAPTER 1
ANTIPASTI: STARTERS

The Italians love to begin their meals with a selection of tasty and colourful dishes. We've combined some of ASK Italian's most popular antipasti with recipes for soups, breads and panini that can also easily be turned into main meals. On the Merenda pages you'll find ideas for dishes to make with children.

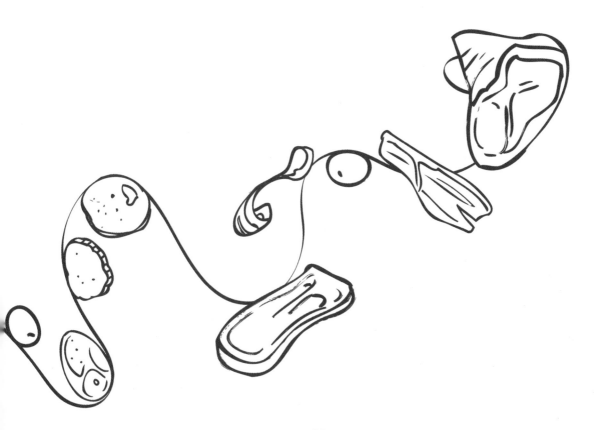

ANTIPASTO CLASSICO

MIXED ANTIPASTI

SERVES 4 / PREP: 10 MINUTES, OR 1 HOUR 30 MINUTES IF YOU MAKE THE
BREAD DOUGH FROM SCRATCH / COOK: 15 MINUTES FOR BAKING THE BREAD

Antipasto means 'before the meal' in Italian, and we've assembled a fabulous selection of different ingredients to make your first course special. This is also an easy way to put together an exciting first course for a dinner party: just arrange the ingredients in pretty dishes and let your guests help themselves. Our antipasti spread is at its best when accompanied by hot, freshly baked ASK Italian Rosemary and Sea Salt Bread (see page 46), but if you don't have time to make it, toast some fresh crusty bread, ciabatta or baguette instead.

2 ASK Italian Rosemary and Sea Salt Breads,
hot from the oven

4 slices Speck (smoked prosciutto)

4 large slices Milano salami

4 large slices fennel salami

4 tablespoons Lilliput or other small capers

200g chargrilled mixed peppers, sliced into large chunks

200g buffalo mozzarella

2 tablespoons ASK Italian extra virgin olive oil

fresh basil leaves, to garnish

4 tablespoons Black Olive Tapenade (see page 45)

freshly ground black pepper

Arrange the ingredients on a large platter or wooden board: group the meats together, then sprinkle the capers over the grilled peppers. Tear the mozzarella to open it slightly and drizzle it with the olive oil before seasoning it with black pepper and basil leaves.

Place the tapenade in a small bowl and serve as a spread with the hot bread.

Adrian recommends: a good Tuscan Rosé such as Argentiera's Bolgheri DOC rosé 2011.

The diverse range of flavours on this mixed antipasti board are perfectly complemented with a crisp, dry Tuscan rosé which has a touch of fruit weight, lean acidity and delicate yet complex flavours.

BRUSCHETTA

SERVES 4-6 / PREP: 20 MINUTES / COOK: 10 MINUTES

Many meals in Italy begin with the simple combination of toasted bread, fruity extra virgin olive oil and a pinch of salt. Bruschetta — the 'ch' is pronounced like a 'k' — can be eaten alone, rubbed with garlic, or topped with other ingredients like tomatoes, mozzarella, prosciutto or goat's cheese. In summer, when the tomatoes are ripe and sweet, rub the bread with the fresh tomato juices. In winter, it's better to choose small or cherry tomatoes. We've enriched our bruschetta topping with sun-dried tomatoes for added flavour.

TOMATO TOPPING:

300g plum tomatoes, de-seeded and chopped

80g (about 15) sun-dried tomatoes in oil, drained and chopped

50g red onion, finely chopped

1 garlic clove, finely chopped

5 fresh basil leaves, finely chopped

a pinch of dried wild oregano

1 tablespoon balsamic vinegar

2 tablespoons ASK Italian extra virgin olive oil

freshly ground sea salt and black pepper

Mix all the ingredients together in a large bowl, season well and set aside for 30 minutes.

BRUSCHETTA:

12 x 1cm slices sourdough, ciabatta or Altamura bread

4 basil leaves, finely chopped

ASK Italian extra virgin olive oil

Toast the bread on both sides under the grill or in a toaster. Arrange the toasts on a serving platter and evenly spoon the tomato mixture onto them. Top with the chopped basil and a drizzle of extra virgin olive oil. Serve immediately.

BRUSCHETTA CON FUNGHI MISTI

BRUSCHETTA WITH MIXED MUSHROOMS

SERVES 4-6 / PREP: 20 MINUTES / COOK: 10 MINUTES

You can also make a great topping for bruschetta with pan-fried mushrooms.

75g (1 medium) portobello mushroom, sliced

100g (4) button mushrooms, sliced

100g (4) chestnut mushrooms sliced

100g (8) oyster mushrooms, sliced

4 tablespoons extra virgin olive oil

1 garlic clove, finely chopped

1 tablespoon chopped thyme

Parmesan, grated (optional)

freshly ground sea salt and black pepper

Sauté the mushrooms together in the oil with the garlic and thyme. Stir to stop the mushrooms from sticking too much. Taste for seasoning. When the mushrooms have softened and are browning slightly, remove from the heat and spoon the mixture onto toasts as above. Top with a little grated cheese if you wish, and with a drizzle of extra virgin olive oil.

ASPARAGI CON SPECK

ASPARAGUS BAKED WITH SMOKED PROSCIUTTO

SERVES 4 / PREP: 15 MINUTES / COOK: 15 MINUTES

This has been a real hit on our Specials menu. It's an easy starter to make in spring when asparagus is in season. Speck is smoked prosciutto or ham, a northern Italian speciality from Alto Adige, and we like the way it complements the sweet flavours of the asparagus. If you can't find Speck, use prosciutto.

24 asparagus spears

4 slices Speck, cut in half lengthways

2 tablespoons ASK Italian extra virgin olive oil

4 handfuls Pangrattato (toasted breadcrumbs), see page 183

Grana Padano or Parmesan cheese, for grating

freshly ground black pepper

Preheat the oven to 220°C/425°F/gas mark 7.

Remove the tough ends of the asparagus. Blanch the spears in a large pan of boiling water for 2–3 minutes, or until just tender. Drain the asparagus and refresh under cold running water.

Wrap the asparagus into bundles with the Speck, three spears at a time. It's easiest if you roll the ham diagonally around the spears.

Arrange the bundles in a shallow baking dish. Drizzle with half the oil and season with black pepper.

Bake in the hot oven for 8 minutes. If you are making the pangrattato at the same time, remember to remove the breadcrumbs from the oven a couple of minutes before the asparagus are done.

Arrange two bundles on each serving plate. Sprinkle with a handful of pangrattato, a few more drops of olive oil and as much grated cheese as you fancy.

INSALATA DI PROSCIUTTO E RUCOLA

CURED HAM AND ROCKET SALAD

SERVES 4 / PREP: 10 MINUTES / COOK: NONE

This tasty layered salad was inspired by one of our teams' trips to a trattoria in Italy. Try making it with Speck, the mildly smoked ham from northern Italy, or with classic Parma ham, known in Italy as prosciutto crudo. The lemon adds a vibrant note to the salad, so be sure to add a good squeeze before serving.

60g (4 good handfuls) rocket leaves

2 tablespoons ASK Italian extra virgin olive oil

12 slices Speck or prosciutto crudo

4 large firm chestnut mushrooms, finely sliced

Grana Padano or Parmesan cheese

1 lemon, cut into 4 wedges

freshly ground sea salt and black pepper

Dress the rocket leaves with the oil in a mixing bowl. Season with freshly ground black pepper and just a pinch of salt.

Arrange the ham slices on a platter or 4 individual serving plates. Cover with the rocket leaves. Top with a layer of sliced raw mushrooms.

Grate as much cheese as you like over the salad. Finish with a squeeze of lemon before serving.

COZZE ALLA MARINARA

MUSSELS IN SPICY TOMATO AND WINE SAUCE

SERVES 4 / PREP: 10 MINUTES / COOK: 15 MINUTES

The 'marinara' in this recipe's title is a sailor's wife: this is how she prepares mussels to give them flavour and Italian appeal. We've taken a page from her book and cook these sweet, fresh mussels in a spicy tomato and white wine sauce that's great to mop up with a chunk of fresh crusty bread.

2 tablespoons ASK Italian extra virgin olive oil

1 garlic clove, finely chopped

600g fresh mussels in the shell

500g tomato passata

1 tablespoon finely chopped fresh flat-leaf parsley

1 tablespoon finely chopped red chilli

1 teaspoon red chilli flakes (optional)

3 tablespoons white wine

4 handfuls Pangrattato (toasted breadcrumbs), see page 183

freshly ground sea salt and black pepper

Heat the olive oil in a large frying pan with a lid. Add the garlic and cook over a medium heat for 1–2 minutes. Add the mussels to the pan, shake the pan well and cover. Cook for 4–6 minutes, or until all the mussels have opened. Discard any that haven't.

Add the tomato passata, parsley, chillies and wine to the mussels. Season with salt and pepper. Turn up the heat and bring the sauce to the boil.

Lower the heat and simmer the sauce, covered, for 10 minutes. Divide between 4 serving bowls, sprinkle with breadcrumbs and serve. Accompany with a green salad of mixed leaves and fennel for a main course.

INVOLTINI DI MELANZANE

AUBERGINE ROLLS

MAKES 8 ROLLS, SERVES 4 / PREP: 35 MINUTES / COOK: 20 MINUTES

This quintessentially summer recipe was given to us by ASK Italian's extra virgin olive oil producers, the Esposito family. They live in Puglia, in the heel of Italy, where the sun brings even aubergines incredible sweetness. Add these rolls to a mixed platter of antipasti, or serve them alone with some fresh mozzarella for a light summer lunch.

2 medium-large aubergines

ASK Italian extra virgin olive oil

90ml tomato passata

dried oregano

80g mozzarella, diced

8 fresh basil leaves, torn into pieces

30g Parmesan or caciocavallo cheese, grated

4 baby plum tomatoes, diced

salt and freshly ground black pepper

Slice the aubergines lengthways into ½cm slices; you should get about 8 good-sized slices. Salt them lightly and stand them in a colander to drip for 20 minutes. Pat dry with paper towels.

Heat 2 tablespoons of extra virgin olive oil in a large heavy frying pan until hot and gradually fry the aubergine slices in the oil for 2 minutes on each side. If you can't fit all the aubergines in one batch, add 2 tablespoons more oil to the pan before cooking the second batch.

Preheat the oven to 180°C/350°F/gas mark 4. In a bowl, season the passata with a pinch of oregano, and salt and pepper to taste. Stir in 2 tablespoons of extra virgin olive oil. Lay each slice of aubergine out on a plate and spread a tablespoonful of the passata over it. Dot with a few cubes of mozzarella, a torn basil leaf and a sprinkling of cheese. Roll each slice of aubergine and arrange the rolls side by side in a shallow baking dish.

Bake for 15 minutes. Serve hot or cold, garnished with the plum tomatoes and a few sprigs of fresh basil.

The Esposito brothers

FRITTATA DI PASTA AVANZATA

FRITTATA OF LEFTOVER PASTA

SERVES 4 / PREP: 10 MINUTES / COOK: 15 MINUTES

Carla says: Frittatas are Italian omelettes. Unlike omelettes, which must be cooked fast over a high heat, frittatas take a more mellow approach and need slow cooking to be at their best. They can be eaten hot or cold, as part of a sandwich filling or on their own with a salad. This frittata is a great way to use up cold leftover pasta, whatever the sauce. You can take a frittata on a picnic or make it for brunch or the kids' supper. They love finding the shape of spaghetti in the eggs.

5–6 large eggs

225–75g cold cooked pasta, with any sauce

50g Parmesan cheese, freshly grated

65g butter

salt and freshly ground black pepper

Beat the eggs lightly with a fork in a medium bowl. Stir in the pasta and the cheese. Season with salt and pepper.

Heat half of the butter in a large non-stick or heavy frying pan. As soon as the foam subsides, pour in the egg mixture. Cook over a moderate heat, without stirring, for 4–5 minutes, or until the bottom is golden brown. Loosen the frittata by shaking the pan backwards and forwards.

Take a large plate, place it upside down over the pan and, holding it firmly with oven gloves, turn the pan and the frittata over onto it. Add the remaining butter to the pan. As soon as it stops foaming slide the frittata back into the pan, and continue cooking for another 3–4 minutes, or until it's golden brown on the second side. Remove from the heat. The frittata can be served hot, at room temperature or cold. Cut into wedges to serve.

MINESTRONE

VEGETABLE SOUP

SERVES 6 / PREP: 20 MINUTES / COOK: 30 MINUTES

Minestrone is Italy's most famous soup. You can make it in any season, using a light vegetable broth in summer and a richer tomato base in autumn and winter. Minestrone's the soup to make when you have a handful of different vegetables and are in the mood for something warm and nutritious. Use your favourite vegetables: it's flexible! Serve with a chunk of fresh bread or with seasoned Italian breadcrumbs, as we have here. If you cut all the vegetables into 1cm dice, they'll cook more evenly. Make a big batch: it's even better the following day.

2 tablespoons ASK Italian extra virgin olive oil

100g leeks, washed carefully and diced

1 medium onion, diced

50g celery, diced

50g carrot, diced

3 garlic cloves, finely chopped

1 x 230g tin chopped tomatoes

300g tomato passata

900ml vegetable stock

1 x 150g tin borlotti beans, rinsed and drained

50g potato, diced

50g courgette, diced

5 fresh basil leaves, sliced

60g baby spinach leaves

1 tablespoon finely chopped fresh flat-leaf parsley

20g Parmesan or Grana Padano cheese, finely grated

salt and freshly ground black pepper

GARNISH:

4 handfuls (30g) Pangrattato (toasted breadcrumbs), see page 183

ASK Italian extra virgin olive oil

Parmesan or Grana Padano cheese

Heat the olive oil in a large saucepan with the leeks, onion, celery, carrot and garlic. Cook for 2–3 minutes over a medium heat to soften the vegetables. Stir in the tomatoes and passata and simmer for another 2–3 minutes. Add the vegetable stock and bring to the boil. Season to taste.

Add the borlotti beans, potatoes and courgettes, cover the pan and cook over a medium to low heat for 20 minutes or until the potatoes soften. You can make the soup in advance up to this point. If you do, bring it back to the boil before continuing with the recipe.

Just before serving, stir in the basil, spinach, parsley and the grated cheese. Mix well and remove from the heat. Allow to stand for 5 minutes before serving in individual bowls. Garnish each serving with a handful of pangrattato and a drizzle of extra virgin olive oil. Serve with a bowl of grated Parmesan or Grana Padano on the side, for sprinkling over the soup.

PAPPA AL POMODORO

TUSCAN TOMATO AND BREAD SOUP
SERVES 6 / PREP: 30 MINUTES / COOK: 10 MINUTES

The Greci family grow the tomatoes that go into our fabulous tomato passata. We asked them for a recipe for this book and they sent a classic farmhouse soup made of… tomatoes! This recipe is as much about the bread as it is about its sun-ripened tomatoes. If you can't find Tuscan bread, use any well-made bread that has a good dense crumb and will keep its structure when wet. This is a classic recipe of the cucina povera, or poor cuisine, created by women who could turn a handful of ripe tomatoes and a piece of stale bread into a magnificent dish. In winter, serve the soup hot. In summer, it can be eaten lukewarm or chilled.

1 kg perfectly ripe fresh tomatoes

6 slices 2-day-old Tuscan or other dense, fine-crumbed bread

8 tablespoons extra virgin olive oil

3 garlic cloves, peeled

300–400ml Vegetable Stock (see page 180)

12 fresh basil leaves

6 tablespoons freshly grated Parmesan cheese

salt and freshly ground black pepper

Bring a small pan of water to the boil. Drop the tomatoes into the water, 2 or 3 at a time, for about 1 minute. Scoop them out with a slotted spoon and, as soon as you can handle them, peel using a small knife. When all the tomatoes have been peeled, pass them through a food mill to separate the seeds and lumps from the juice and pulp. If you don't have a food mill, use a food processor to whizz the tomatoes, then push them through a sieve to remove the seeds. The combined pulp and juice is called passata.

Toast the bread lightly. Rub 2 of the garlic cloves over the bread, just enough to flavour the slices. Cut the toast into 3cm squares.

In a saucepan, heat half the oil with the remaining garlic clove. When the garlic begins to take on colour but before it browns, stir in the tomato passata. Bring to the boil. Add the bread and stir, using a whisk. Slowly pour in 300ml of the broth, mixing to break up the bread. If you prefer a less dense soup, add 100ml more of the broth. Season with salt and pepper. Bring the soup back up to the boil over a medium heat. When the bread has dissolved, remove from the heat. Discard the garlic. Serve hot or allow to cool before serving.

Divide the soup between 6 serving bowls. Swirl the remaining extra virgin olive oil onto each serving, top with a couple of basil leaves and a spoonful of grated cheese, and serve.

The Greci brothers

PASTA E CECI

PASTA AND CHICKPEA SOUP

SERVES 4-6 / PREP: OVERNIGHT SOAKING + 15 MINUTES / COOK: 2 HOURS 30 MINUTES

Carla says: Pulses like chickpeas and lentils are very popular in Italian cooking. They grow well in central and southern Italy and are great sources of protein. Here chickpeas and pasta are scented with the quintessential Mediterranean herb, rosemary.

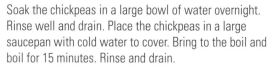

200g dried chickpeas

3 garlic cloves, peeled

1 bay leaf

6 tablespoons extra virgin olive oil

½ a dried chilli pepper, crumbled, or to taste

50g pancetta or bacon, diced

a sprig of fresh rosemary

600ml water

150g ditalini or other short hollow pasta

Parmesan cheese, freshly grated (optional)

salt

Soak the chickpeas in a large bowl of water overnight. Rinse well and drain. Place the chickpeas in a large saucepan with cold water to cover. Bring to the boil and boil for 15 minutes. Rinse and drain.

Return the chickpeas to the pan. Add water to cover, 1 garlic clove, the bay leaf, 3 tablespoons of the oil and the chilli. Simmer until tender, about 2 hours, adding more water as necessary.

Remove the bay leaf. Process half of the chickpeas through a food mill or purée in a food processor with a few tablespoons of the cooking liquid. Return the purée to the pan with the rest of the chickpeas and the remaining cooking water.

In a small frying pan, sauté the diced pork gently in the remaining oil with the rosemary sprig and 2 remaining garlic cloves until just golden. Remove and discard the rosemary and garlic. Add the pork with its oils to the chickpeas.

Add 600ml water to the chickpeas and bring to the boil. Taste for seasoning. Stir in the pasta and cook until just al dente. Let the soup stand for about 5 minutes before serving with the cheese on the side.

WHITE BEAN AND SUN-DRIED TOMATO DIP

SERVES 4-5 / PREP: 20 MINUTES / COOK: NONE

Carla says: Next time you're looking for a quick dip to make, try this easy, one-stop blender recipe. It's great with raw vegetables or garlic bread sticks. If you can't find plain sun-dried tomatoes, use them preserved in oil, adding enough extra water to reach a smooth consistency.

4 sun-dried tomatoes

1 x 400g tin cannellini beans, rinsed and drained

2 tablespoons extra virgin olive oil

1 tablespoon fresh lemon juice

1 garlic clove

¼ teaspoon cayenne pepper (optional)

salt and freshly ground black pepper

Place the sun-dried tomatoes in a small bowl. Cover with boiling water and leave to soften for about 15 minutes.

Put all the other ingredients in the bowl of a food processor. Add the tomatoes and a little of their steeping water. Process to a purée. Add more water as necessary. Taste for seasoning. Refrigerate until needed.

BLACK OLIVE TAPENADE

MAKES APPROX. 450G (22 TABLESPOONS) / PREP: 15 MINUTES / COOK: NONE

Tapenade is only as good as the olives you use in it, so choose your favourites, whether they are the small sweet black olives from Liguria, Gaeta or Provence, or the saltier, more intensely flavoured Kalamata olives. For an even more intense sauce, add a few anchovies to the bowl before mixing. This is such a useful condiment. At ASK Italian we use it to top pastas and pizzas, or to accompany our Rosemary and Sea Salt Bread (see page 46), which is great with a glass of wine before dinner.

250g black olives, pitted and finely chopped

1 tablespoon small capers, drained and finely chopped

2 garlic cloves, crushed with a little sea salt

10g fresh basil leaves, finely chopped

zest and juice of ½ a lemon

185ml ASK Italian extra virgin olive oil

freshly ground black pepper

Put the olives, capers, garlic, basil and lemon zest into a bowl and, using a hand blender, blend until you have a smooth paste. Add the lemon juice and olive oil and mix well. Season with black pepper to taste.

Tapenade keeps well in the fridge for up to one month in an air-tight container.

ROSEMARY AND SEA SALT BREAD

SERVES 4 / PREP: UP TO 2 HOURS / COOK: UP TO 15 MINUTES

Pizza dough makes amazing breads! We have created this focaccia-style bread using our pizza dough. It features in ASK Italian panini and is great with salads and antipasti.

4 pizza dough balls, 170g each (made from 1 Basic Pizza Dough recipe; see page 106)

semolina or strong flour for dusting

8 tablespoons ASK Italian extra virgin olive oil

2 tablespoons roughly chopped fresh rosemary leaves

freshly ground sea salt and black pepper

Preheat the oven to 220°C/425°F/gas mark 7.

Dust the worktop and the dough balls with a little semolina or flour. Stretch each dough ball into a 10–12cm oval shape.

Place on a well-oiled baking tray. Brush or drizzle the top of each bread evenly with 1 tablespoon of oil. Sprinkle with the rosemary. Season with salt and pepper. Use your fingers to lightly press the rosemary and salt into the top of the breads.

Bake for 12–15 minutes or until the bread has puffed and browned. Remove from the oven and brush with the remaining oil. Let the oil sink in for 30 seconds before you serve the bread.

PANINO DI POLLO

CHICKEN PANINO

SERVES 2 / PREP: 2 HOURS IF YOU ARE BAKING THE BREAD; 15 MINUTES IF YOU
USE READY-MADE BREAD / COOK: 30 MINUTES

This hot sandwich is a meal in itself, especially if you serve it with a side salad. If you don't have time to bake your own bread, use a baguette or two slices of sourdough bread.

2 chicken breasts, skin removed

2 tablespoons ASK Italian extra virgin olive oil

2 Rosemary and Sea Salt Breads, hot from the oven (see previous page)

2 tablespoons Salsa Verde (see page 182)

15g rocket leaves

1 medium tomato, sliced

salt and freshly ground black pepper

To butterfly the chicken place one chicken breast on a cutting board. With a sharp knife, cut the breast horizontally, leaving a 1cm strip along the long edge of the breast uncut. Now you'll be able to flip the top open, like two pages of a book joined at the seam. Repeat with the second breast.

Heat the oil in a non-stick frying pan large enough to hold both breasts open. Cook the chicken for 2 minutes on each side, turning it only once. Check that it is cooked through by making a little incision in the thickest part and, if necessary, cook for a minute or two more. Don't overcook it or the chicken will dry out. Remove from the pan and allow the meat to rest for a minute before slicing into chunky strips.

Cut the bread in half lengthways and open out. Spread the salsa verde on both sides of the bread. Stack the bottom slice with rocket, tomato and chicken. Cover with the other slice of bread and cut the panino in half before serving.

PANINO DI PORTOBELLO

MUSHROOM AND CHEESE PANINO

SERVES 1 / PREP: 2 HOURS IF YOU ARE BAKING THE BREAD; 15 MINUTES IF YOU
USE READY-MADE BREAD / COOK: 15 MINUTES

Portobello mushrooms are a tasty alternative to meat as they are full of flavour and have great texture. This recipe is for just one person, but it's easy to double or triple the ingredients for more of this delicious panino.

1 large portobello mushroom, stalk removed

1 tablespoon ASK Italian extra virgin olive oil

a pinch of chopped fresh thyme

30g Fontal or Gruyère cheese, thinly sliced

1 Rosemary and Sea Salt Bread, hot from the oven
(see page 46), or use a baguette or your favourite bread

2 tablespoons Salsa Verde (see page 182)

15 rocket leaves

½ a medium tomato, sliced

salt and freshly ground black pepper

Preheat the oven to 200°C/400°F/gas mark 6.

Place the mushroom in a small baking dish, stalk-side up. Drizzle with the oil and season with thyme, salt and pepper. Arrange thin slices of Fontal over the mushroom. Bake for 10–12 minutes, or until the mushroom has softened and the cheese has melted. Allow to cool for 1 minute before slicing into 1.5cm strips.

Cut the bread in half lengthways and open it out. Spread the salsa verde on both sides of the bread. Arrange the rocket and tomato on the bottom half of the bread and top with the cheesy mushroom slices. Cover with the other slice of bread and cut in half before serving.

MERENDA

CHILDREN'S SNACKS

Carla says: Merenda is the Italian word for a mid-morning or mid-afternoon snack, usually for children. Italian children eat lunch very late, so they are often sent to school with a piece of pizza or focaccia in their backpack for their mid-morning merenda, or they are given a healthy fruit frullato (like a smoothie) or fresh vegetables to keep them going in the afternoon. Here are some simple ideas of things you can make with your kids to keep them eating well.

FRULLATO

Frullare is the Italian verb for blending, and this Italian smoothie blends fresh fruits with ice for a refreshing healthy drink. It doesn't usually contain milk, yogurt or sugar, but you can add them if you prefer, along with a little vanilla extract or honey.

All you do to make a frullato is put a few of your favourite fruits into the blender with some ice and blend. Serve with a straw.

Here are some popular Italian combinations to get you started:

Peach, banana and blueberry

Strawberry, apricot and apple

Fig, banana and apple

GRILLED CHEESE CROSTINI

Here's an original way to make a snack that will keep your kids busy while they help you. Cut day-old white or brown bread with cookie cutters and top with your favourite cheese. Add a little piece of olive, anchovy, grilled pepper or capers for added flavour. Grill for 10 minutes or until the cheese melts.

PINZIMONIO

Italians often start their meals with a lovely arrangement of raw and blanched vegetables that goes beyond just carrot and celery sticks.

Try slicing fennel bulbs, raw peppers, radishes, carrots, cucumber and celery and arranging them around your favourite dip. The Italians usually just use really fresh and fruity extra virgin olive oil with a pinch of salt and pepper. You can also choose from our dressings on page 178. For added flavour try scooping out cherry tomatoes and filling them with a spoonful of Pesto alla Genovese (see page 179).

WE LOVE ITALIAN!

Great Ormond Street Hospital for Children is lucky to have a host of very special friends who share our love of Italian food. We asked them about their favourite Italian food experiences.

GINO D'ACAMPO

Why do you love Italian food?

The question here should be: why wouldn't anyone love Italian food? It's good for you, filling yet not fattening, full of healthy, seasonal, natural ingredients and simply delicious. You can never tire of it; there are so many varieties. People also have the misconception that Italian food is bad if you're watching your weight, yet the Italians are the healthiest people in Europe!

What are your favourite eating experiences in Italy?

There is nothing better than a huge seafood pasta platter on the coast of southern Italy, simply cooked with some white wine. A close second would be Nutella ice-cream in a piazza in any region. Tasting cheese and wines in Bologna and pizza in Naples are musts. Eating at an agriturismo, or rural farm, with no menu and five daily dishes accompanied by home-made wine is a culinary experience everyone should try.

Do your children like Italian food? What's their favourite?

I'm very lucky that my children love all cuisines. We have a rule in our house that you don't have to like or finish it, but you do have to try it. Of course their favourite food is Italian. My youngest would go for pizza topped with salame or mortadella every day of the week, whereas my oldest would choose pasta or meat dishes.

RONNI ANCONA

Why do you love Italian food?

I love Italian food because, when cooked well, it is sublimely delicious and sensuous. Sadly, my own Italian cooking doesn't quite fit that description!

What are your favourite eating experiences in Italy?

The Norcia lentils from Umbria are very special as are the tomatoes in Sicily. Linguine with seafood is my idea of heaven.

Do your children like Italian food? What's their favourite?

They love pasta, especially the fresh variety. Forget the proper name, they like 'the curly one' with just a bit of butter and cheese.

Photo: Giles Keyte

DAME HELEN MIRREN

Why do you love Italian food?

I love Italian food because of the local nature of it. You only eat what is locally grown and the cuisine changes every 20 miles or so.

What are your favourite eating experiences in Italy?

I love to eat the 'crudo', or raw fish, in the Salento area of southern Italy where I have a house. This coastal area is famous for its seafood. There is also a marvellous local dish called fave e cicoria, which is mashed up dried fava beans eaten with the green tops of bitter wild chicory. Very basic, local and delicious. The food and wine in Puglia in general is extremely good.

Photo: Simon Songhurst

CLAUDIA WINKLEMAN

Why do you love Italian food?

I ADORE Italian food. I get excited about anything on my plate but Italian food is so delicious and when made really simply, there's nothing better. Did I mention minestrone? A good bowl of Italian soup makes me want to punch the air.

What are your favourite eating experiences in Italy?

I prefer simple places. Lots of knives and forks and men in white gloves make me nervous. The best food I've ever had in Italy and perhaps in my life has been in town squares (don't get me started on town squares, they're the greatest places to watch and live life). Eating something straightforward like a pizza or a big bowl of pasta. Nobody does it quite like the Italians. Whether you're in a square in Venice, Pisa or Bologna or on the Amalfi coast, it's all about local delicious simple food. And tomatoes. They're very good with um, tomatoes. I should also add that I'm very keen on Italian ice cream. VERY.

Do your children like Italian food? What's their favourite?

They love pasta and Parmesan cheese more than anything. Sometimes when we're running late and they're hungry I'll just break off a hunk of sharp, salty Parmesan cheese for them to nibble on til they feel normal again.

FLAVIA CACACE

Why do you love Italian food?

I love Italian food because it's based on simple healthy ingredients. You know what you're eating and can appreciate the flavours. It's also not that time consuming to prepare.

What are your favourite eating experiences in Italy?

My favourite Italian cake is called il babà and I have great memories of eating one every night when I was on holiday. It's very hard to find in the UK, thank heavens.

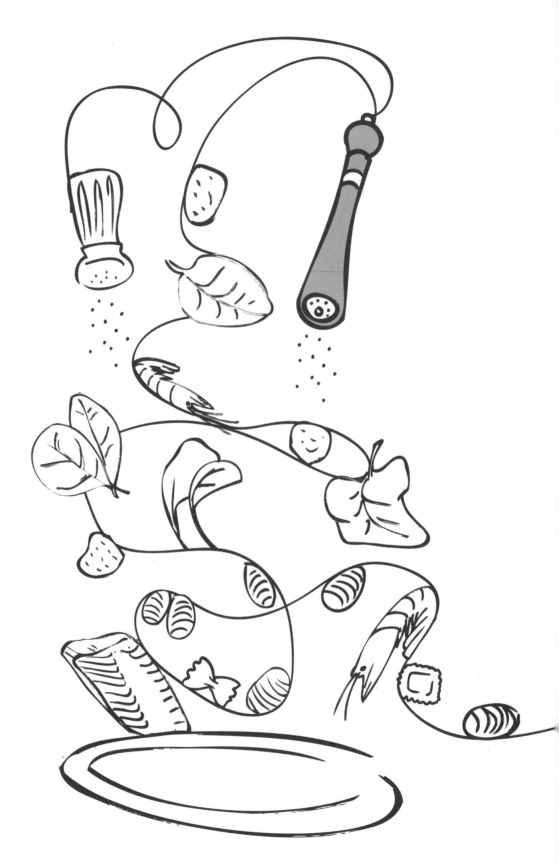

CHAPTER 2
PRIMI: PASTA

Our pasta chapter starts with lots of great recipes for dried pasta, like spaghetti, linguine and penne. It's followed by instructions for making your own egg pasta and by recipes for noodles and lasagne.

20 QUESTIONS ABOUT PASTA

Pasta is easy to cook, we all know that. But there's a big difference between spaghetti swimming in a roomy pan or jammed into a tiny saucepan in just an inch of water. The taste and the texture will be completely different. Here are Carla's answers to the questions she is asked most often about how to cook perfect pasta.

1 WHICH PASTA TO CHOOSE?

Look for imported Italian pasta which is now easy to find in the UK. It is made with the right kinds of flour and has been produced to hold its bite when cooked and not go mushy. ASK Italian always uses De Cecco, one of Italy's most iconic and favourite pasta producers. Their pasta is made with the prestigious bronze dies that give the pasta better texture.

2 HOW MUCH WATER TO BOIL?

Choose a big or very big pan and fill it three-quarters full of water. The pasta should have lots of room to move around in so the water doesn't get too starchy. Use at least one litre per person.

3 WHEN TO SALT?

Add the salt once the water is simmering. Then bring it to a rapid boil. Use about 1½ tablespoons of salt to 500g of pasta. If you don't salt the water, the pasta will taste bland.

4 WHEN TO PUT THE PASTA IN?

The water should be boiling rapidly when you drop the pasta in. Stir it to stop it clumping. Then stir occasionally as it cooks. Never add oil to the pan as it makes the pasta stickier and interferes with the sauce.

5 WHEN TO TAKE THE PASTA OUT?

The Italians like their pasta quite firm. The best rule is to follow the packet instructions but start tasting small pieces of pasta when you are within 2 minutes of the suggested cooking time. Then it's up to your own preferences. If you are finishing the pasta by cooking it in the sauce, take it out when it's a little underdone.

6 WHAT IS AL DENTE?

This phrase means 'firm to the bite'. Cooked this way, the pasta's 'soul' – its innermost part – stays firm and doesn't go limp or gummy. The outer part of the pasta will be soft, but the core still chewy.

7 HOW TO TAKE IT OUT?

Most people use a colander to drain their pasta. Theo Randall prefers to use pasta tongs or a strainer to pull the pasta out of the water so it doesn't get compressed in the colander. Never rinse pasta under water after it's been cooked. Don't over-drain the pasta: a bit of water with it will stop it drying out too much. Move quickly as it should be eaten hot.

8 SHOULD YOU THROW AWAY ALL THE COOKING WATER?

No. Before you drain the pasta, remove a mugful of the hot pasta cooking water and set it aside for use later in the sauce.

9 WHAT SHAPE OF PASTA FOR YOUR SAUCE?

Generally, chunky sauces go well with short pasta whose holes and grooves can trap the sauce better. Smoother sauces go better with long pasta. Beyond that, it's great to find your own favourite combinations.

10 HOW MUCH PASTA TO COOK?

That depends on your appetite, but as a general rule, 60–80g per person is fine for an appetizer portion; 90–120g produces larger or main course portions.

11 HOW MUCH SAUCE TO USE?

The Italians don't like their pasta to be swimming in sauce. It should be evenly covered but not dripping. For them, it's as much about the flavours of the pasta as it is about the sauce.

12 WHAT'S THE DIFFERENCE BETWEEN EGG PASTA AND DRIED?

Dried pasta is best made from durum or hard wheat. Egg pasta is made from soft flour and eggs. They result in very different textures and tastes.

13 WHY USE EGG PASTA?

Egg pasta (pasta all'uovo), or noodles, is more elastic and tastes of egg as much as flour. It is even better made fresh, and can be made by hand and rolled with a rolling pin or in a pasta machine (see page 72).

14 WHY USE DRY PASTA?

Pastasciutta, as it is called in Italy, contains only water and flour and is extruded by a powerful press through holes or dies that are designed to produce spaghetti, linguine, penne or dozens of other shapes, each with its own texture and character.

15 IF MY PASTA SAUCE IS TOO THICK, SHOULD I ADD OIL?

No, try adding the reserved cooking water from the pasta. It already has some pasta flavour and will not make your sauce heavier.

16 HOW TO FINISH COOKING THE PASTA?

The most authentic way is to make your sauce in a large frying pan big enough to hold the pasta after it is cooked. Keep the sauce hot while you cook the pasta and turn it into the sauce after draining. Then cook over a medium heat, stirring, until the sauce and pasta are well blended. Add cooking water as needed. You'll find the flavours are much better than when the sauce is added to the pasta in a bowl.

17 IS THERE A HURRY ABOUT SERVING PASTA?

Yes! The Italians say that the pasta waits for no one. So make sure all your guests are ready to eat before cooking the pasta. It must be eaten steaming hot to get the best out of it.

18 WHAT ABOUT LEFTOVER PASTA?

Pasta can be reheated with a bit of water or extra sauce, though it will never be as good as the first time around. It keeps in the fridge for a day or two, and is also good cold. Or try making a pasta frittata (see page 38). Cover lasagne with foil to stop it drying out too much, and reheat in the oven until hot all the way through.

19 HOW ABOUT A PASTA SALAD?

For a cold pasta salad, cook the pasta as usual but when it is done add a bit of olive oil and keep stirring until it cools, then dress it.

20 CAN I BAKE PASTA?

If you are making short pasta that will be finished in the oven (such as our rigatoni, see page 68), remember to undercook the pasta by 3 or 4 minutes in the boiling water before you mix it with a bit more sauce than usual. The pasta will go on soaking up the sauce as it bakes.

SPAGHETTI AL POMODORO

SPAGHETTI WITH TOMATO SAUCE

SERVES 4-6 / PREP: 15 MINUTES / COOK: 20 MINUTES

Italians eat an incredible 30 kilograms each of pasta per year, and spaghetti al pomodoro makes up a big percentage of that pasta mountain. Kids love it too, so it's become a staple in households all over the world. We like to top ours with mozzarella for a creamier, fresher tasting result.

4 tablespoons ASK Italian extra virgin olive oil

3 garlic cloves, finely chopped

230g plum tomatoes, de-seeded and quartered

1 x 400g tin chopped tomatoes

500g tomato passata

12 basil leaves, finely chopped

500g De Cecco or other Italian spaghetti

200g buffalo mozzarella, torn into bite-size pieces

salt and freshly ground black pepper

Bring a large pan of salted water to the rolling boil for the pasta.

Heat 2 tablespoons of the oil in a large saucepan over a low heat. Add the chopped garlic and cook for 1–2 minutes. Stir in the fresh tomatoes and cook for 2 minutes, until they start to soften.

Add the tinned tomatoes and the passata with half the basil, stirring as you bring the sauce to the boil. Season to taste with salt and pepper. Lower the heat and simmer gently for 10 minutes.

Meanwhile, cook the spaghetti according to the packet instructions. Drain when al dente and turn the pasta into a heated bowl. Stir in half of the sauce and mix well. Serve the pasta in individual bowls, topped with a spoonful of the remaining sauce, the torn mozzarella pieces, a drizzle of extra virgin olive oil and a pinch of chopped basil.

 Adrian recommends: ASK Italian's Merlot Veronese.

This is a lovely, light pasta dish that combines fresh tomato, herbs and buffalo mozzarella. I've paired it with a crisp, young red wine with refreshing acidity and a similar level of flavour intensity.

LINGUINE ALLA GENOVESE

LINGUINE WITH PESTO, BEANS AND POTATOES

SERVES 4 AS A MAIN COURSE / PREP: 15 MINUTES / COOK: 15 MINUTES

In Genoa, on the Italian Riviera, the locals love to add green beans and potatoes to make their pesto sauce more special. We use waxy British new potatoes like Charlottes. Jerzy Jozefiak, our Head Chef in Cheltenham, has this tip: 'Cook your potatoes and beans first so you can quickly add them to the sauce.'

4 tablespoons ASK Italian extra virgin olive oil

400g new potatoes such as Charlottes, cooked, peeled and sliced

200g green beans, blanched for 2 minutes in boiling water

125ml single cream

250ml water

200ml Pesto alla Genovese (see page 179), plus 60ml (4 tablespoons) to serve

500g De Cecco or other Italian linguine

4 sprigs of fresh basil

salt and freshly ground black pepper

Bring a large pan of salted water to the rolling boil for the pasta.

Heat the oil in a frying pan over low heat. Add the sliced potatoes and cook for 2–3 minutes until they start to turn golden. Stir in the green beans, cream, water and the pesto. Gently bring the sauce to the boil. Season lightly with salt and pepper. Reduce the heat and simmer for 2 minutes, taking care not to let the cream separate.

Cook the linguine according to packet instructions. Drain.

Turn the linguine into the pesto sauce and cook together gently for 1–2 minutes. Divide the pasta between hot serving bowls, top each with a spoonful of green pesto and a sprig of basil, and serve.

LINGUINE CON FRUTTI DI MARE

LINGUINE WITH SEAFOOD SAUCE

SERVES 4-6 / PREP: 15 MINUTES / COOK: 20 MINUTES

Nothing reminds us more of a summer lunch at the Italian seaside than this great pasta dish, studded with all our favourite seafood. Claudio Rodrigues-Baltasar, our Head Chef in Truro, is happy it's on the main menu: 'Everyone loves fish, especially here in Cornwall.'

2 tablespoons ASK Italian extra virgin olive oil

1 garlic clove, finely chopped

180g clams in their shells, scrubbed

160g mussels in their shells, scrubbed

180g king prawns

140g squid, cut into rings

1 x 400g tin chopped tomatoes

500g passata

60ml (4 tablespoons) white wine

4 tablespoons finely chopped fresh flat-leaf parsley

100ml fish stock

juice of 1 medium lemon

500g De Cecco or other Italian linguine

freshly ground sea salt and black pepper

Bring a large pan of salted water to the rolling boil for the pasta.

Heat the oil in a large frying pan over a low heat. Add the garlic and cook for 1–2 minutes, taking care the garlic doesn't burn. Add the clams and mussels and cook for 2–3 minutes, shaking the pan to heat the shellfish evenly. Discard any that do not open. Stir in the prawns and squid and cook for a further minute.

Add the chopped tomatoes, passata, white wine, half of the parsley, fish stock and lemon juice. Gently bring the sauce to the boil. Season to taste with salt and pepper, reduce the heat and gently simmer for 10 minutes.

Cook the linguine according to packet instructions until it is almost al dente. Use a mug to scoop out some of the hot pasta cooking water. Set aside.

Drain the pasta and turn it into the pan with the seafood sauce. Gently stir the pasta into the sauce over a medium heat. Cook for 2–3 minutes, adding a little of the hot cooking water if the sauce seems too dry. Sprinkle with the remaining parsley and serve on hot plates.

SPAGHETTI ALLA CARBONARA

SPAGHETTI WITH PANCETTA, EGGS AND CHEESE

SERVES 6 / PREP: 10 MINUTES / COOK: 20 MINUTES

This classic Roman dish divides the culinary world: most Italians say it shouldn't include cream, while others prefer adding cream. Theo Randall simply calls it egg and bacon pasta and rustles it up for family brunches — without the cream. (If you want cream, we'll tell you when to add it.) The secret to cooking the eggs enough is to have them at room temperature and to heat the mixing and serving bowls. If you prefer bacon to pancetta, use unsmoked bacon. Have all your ingredients ready before you cook the pasta.

250g pancetta or guanciale, cubed

1 teaspoon ASK Italian extra virgin olive oil

500g De Cecco or other Italian spaghetti

6 large egg yolks, at room temperature

100g Parmesan or Grana Padano cheese, finely grated

100g pecorino Romano cheese, finely grated

2 tablespoons finely chopped fresh flat-leaf parsley

50ml single cream, at room temperature (optional)

freshly ground sea salt and black pepper

Bring a large pan of salted water to the rolling boil for the pasta.

Sauté the pancetta slowly in a small frying pan with a teaspoon of oil until the pork has rendered its fat and is becoming golden and crispy. Turn off the heat but leave the pancetta in the pan.

Drop the spaghetti into the boiling water and cook according to package instructions.

When the pasta is almost cooked, place the egg yolks in a large warm serving bowl and stir in three-quarters of both cheeses and a tablespoon and a half of parsley. Grind in some black pepper. Turn the heat on under the pancetta pan to keep it hot.

Just before draining the pasta, use a mug to scoop out some of the hot pasta cooking water. Set it aside.

Tip the steaming, drained pasta immediately into the bowl with the eggs and stir to coat the pasta and cook the eggs.

Add half a mugful of the hot pasta cooking water. Top with the pancetta and its hot oil and stir again. (If you want to add cream, do it now.)

Serve the carbonara immediately, garnished with parsley and black pepper, and with the rest of the grated cheese on the side.

PENNE CON SALSICCIA E PORCINI

PENNE WITH ITALIAN SAUSAGE, PORCINI MUSHROOMS AND TOMATO

SERVES 4 / PREP: 10 MINUTES / COOK: 35 MINUTES

Theo says: This pasta dish is delicious because the Italian sausages have lots of flavour, making the sauce rich and comforting. If you can't find aged pecorino, use Parmesan cheese.

4 tablespoons extra virgin olive oil

1 small red onion, chopped

1 garlic clove, chopped

200g Italian sausages, skins removed

50g dried porcini, soaked in a cup of warm water

1 x 400g tin chopped plum tomatoes

50ml double cream

400g penne rigate

50g dried porcini mushrooms, soaked

pecorino stagionato cheese, to grate

salt and freshly ground black pepper

Bring a large pan of salted water to the boil for the pasta.

Heat the oil in a large saucepan over a low heat. Add the onion and garlic and cook for 3–4 minutes, stirring, until the onion softens.

Meanwhile, chop the sausage meat. When the onions are soft, add the meat to the pan, stir and cook over a medium heat for 10 minutes. Remove the mushrooms from their soaking water and chop, reserving the water. Add the mushrooms and water to the meat in the pan.

Drain off excess fat, add the tomatoes and cook for 20 minutes. Finish by adding the double cream, keeping the sauce at a simmer. Taste for seasoning.

Meanwhile, cook the penne according to packet instructions. Drain. Turn the pasta into the pan with the hot sauce and mix well over a low heat. Serve the pasta with pecorino stagionato to grate at the table.

RIGATONI CON MANZO PICCANTE

RIGATONI WITH SPICY BEEF SAUCE

SERVES 4-6 / PREP: 30 MINUTES / COOK: 40 MINUTES

Spice up your Bolognese sauce for this hearty winter warmer, which is finished in the oven.

4 tablespoons ASK Italian extra virgin olive oil

½ a garlic clove, finely chopped

250g (around 22) small lean beef meatballs, preferably with herbs added

120g Balsamic Onions (see page 179)

20g (2 tablespoons) green chilli, de-seeded and finely chopped, or to taste

100g roasted red peppers, thinly sliced

115g tomato passata

450g Bolognese Sauce (see page 181)

60ml (4 tablespoons) white wine

500g De Cecco Rigatoncello no 28 or other short Italian pasta

50g mozzarella cheese, grated or cubed

Parmesan or Grana Padano cheese, for grating

½ teaspoon paprika

salt and freshly ground black pepper

Bring a large pan of salted water to the boil for the pasta. Preheat the oven to 220°C/425°F/gas mark 7.

Heat the oil in a large frying pan over a low heat. Add the chopped garlic and sauté gently for 2 minutes, taking care not to let it burn. Add the meatballs. Cook for 3–4 minutes until evenly browned, turning the meatballs with a wooden spoon. Add the wine and cook until the liquid evaporates.

Stir in the balsamic onions, green chilli, peppers, passata and Bolognese sauce. Slowly bring the sauce to a boil. Season to taste with salt and pepper. Reduce the heat and simmer for 2–3 minutes.

Drop the pasta into the boiling water and stir well. Cook for 2 minutes less than the packet instructions, until the pasta is barely al dente. It will finish cooking in the oven. Drain the pasta and stir it into the pan with the sauce. Cook gently for 2 minutes.

Turn the pasta into an ovenproof dish. Sprinkle the top with the mozzarella and grated Parmesan or Grana Padano. Bake for 10 to 15 minutes, or until the cheese has melted and browned. Sprinkle with paprika before serving.

PENNE AL POLLO DELLA CASA

CHICKEN WITH PENNE PASTA

SERVES 4-6 / PREP: 40 MINUTES / COOK: 15 MINUTES

Jeena Rodrigues, ASK Italian's Head of Food, says: This baked pasta dish is a favourite among customers and team members at ASK Italian. It combines pasta, chicken and mushrooms in a creamy, thyme-scented white wine sauce. It's a great dish for a family Sunday lunch.

4 tablespoons ASK Italian extra virgin olive oil

300g button mushrooms, sliced

400g raw chicken breasts, cut into thin strips

30g butter

60ml dry white wine

375g Salsa di Funghi (half the recipe) (see page 180)

380ml single cream

1 tablespoon finely chopped fresh thyme

500g De Cecco or other Italian penne

40g Parmesan or Grana Padano cheese, grated

freshly ground sea salt and black pepper

2 sprigs of fresh thyme, to garnish

Heat 3 tablespoons of the oil in a medium frying pan. Add the mushrooms and sauté over a medium heat for 3–4 minutes or until they start to soften. Remove from the heat and set aside.

Toss the chicken pieces in a bowl with 1 tablespoon of oil. Season with salt and pepper.

Bring a large pan of salted water to a rolling boil for the pasta. Preheat the oven to 200°C/400°F/gas mark 6.

Melt the butter in a large saucepan. When it foams, add the chicken pieces, turning them to brown evenly on all sides for 3–4 minutes. Stir in the wine, raise the heat and cook until the wine has evaporated. Add the sautéed mushrooms, mushroom sauce, cream and thyme to the pan. Stir as you bring the sauce gently to the boil. Lower the heat and simmer for 10 minutes.

Cook the pasta for 2 minutes less than the package instructions. Drain. Turn the penne into the pan with the sauce and cook together for 1–2 minutes. Spoon the pasta mixture into an ovenproof dish. Sprinkle with the cheese. Bake for 10–15 minutes, or until the top is beginning to brown. Remove from the oven, garnish with the thyme and serve with a mixed salad.

HOW TO MAKE FRESH PASTA

It's really not difficult to make home-made pasta, especially if you use your food processor and a manual pasta machine to crank the pasta. You'll taste the difference and with fresh pasta you can make your own lasagne and filled pastas such as ravioli.

We wanted our teams across the country to understand how fresh pasta is made, so as part of our Italian education programme we recently took to the road with Theo as our guide. They had a great time mixing, rolling, cutting and eating it!

Pasta is made from just flour and eggs. Look for Italian '00' flour, which is very finely ground, or strong flour if you can't find it. Use good organic eggs. If you want to make your pasta a bit richer, add one extra egg yolk for each 100g of flour. Pasta-making is an inexact science as egg sizes and flours can vary, but you can always adjust it by adding a little more flour or a few drops of water if needed.

After it has been mixed, the dough needs to be proved, which replaces hand kneading. You can do this in the pasta machine. If you are making ravioli or other stuffed pasta, make the dough on the day you are going to serve it. Ribbon pasta, such as fettuccine or tagliatelle, can be made several hours or a day in advance: the pasta needs time to dry a little before being cooked.

As a general rule, these are the quantities you'll need in order to make the dough for our noodle recipes. For lasagne quantities, follow the instructions given in the individual recipes.

FOR 3–4 PEOPLE:

3 large eggs

250g '00' or strong flour

50g fine semolina flour

FOR 5–6 PEOPLE:

4 large eggs

325g '00' or strong flour

75g fine semolina flour

If you want to make larger quantities, do it in two batches or the dough will not fit in the food processor. If you are making a larger amount, make the dough as below but cut it into 3 or 4 balls before proving it.

MAKING THE DOUGH:

Place all the ingredients in the bowl of a food processor and pulse until a ball of dough is formed. It should feel smooth to the touch, firm but with a slightly sticky texture. If the dough feels too moist, add another spoonful of flour.

Remove the dough and divide it into 2 balls. Cover them with clingfilm so they don't dry out. The dough can be refrigerated at this point, and will keep for up to 10 days.

PROVING THE DOUGH:

Set the rollers of your pasta machine at their widest setting. Pass the dough through the machine as you turn the handle. Fold the pasta in three. Give the roller setting one-quarter turn to narrow the rollers and pass the dough through the machine again, then fold in three again. Repeat at least 3 more times, narrowing the rollers each time. By now the glutens in the flour will have been kneaded and will be elastic. Make the pasta as thin as you feel comfortable working with. The pasta sheet should be no longer than 60cm or it will be difficult to handle and may break.

CUTTING THE DOUGH:

To make noodles, pass the dough sheet through one of the cutting settings, either wide or narrow. Lift the cut pasta ribbons and form them into little loose nests by turning your wrist as you place the pasta down. Allow to dry for at least 2 hours before using.

TO MAKE PASTA FOR LASAGNE:

Roll the dough to the next to last setting (not the thinnest) and cut the sheets into lengths the same size as your baking dish. Sprinkle a bit of semolina flour onto a clean surface and lay the pasta sheets onto it while you prepare to cook them. Do not allow the dough to dry out. You can always cover the pasta with a damp tea cloth if necessary. For lasagne quantities, use the specific amounts you'll find in the recipes, then follow the instructions on these pages.

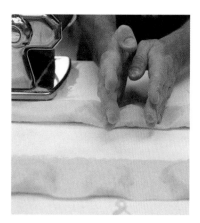  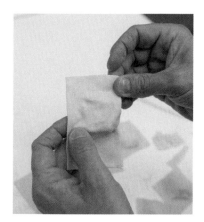

TO MAKE RAVIOLI:

Prepare the filling before making the dough. Roll the dough to the next to last setting (not the thinnest) in lengths of about 60cm. Do not let the pasta dry out before filling it. Sprinkle a little semolina flour on a clean work surface or wooden board.

If your pasta machine makes strips of pasta 12–15cm wide, lay a 60cm length of pasta down on a flat board. Drop small teaspoonfuls of filling along the pasta with 4cm between them. Brush the area between the filling with a little water and fold the pasta sheet over onto itself, pressing gently with your fingers to seal and to avoid trapping air pockets in the ravioli. Use a fluted pastry wheel or sharp knife to cut between the filling to form the ravioli.

If your pasta strips are less than 12cm wide, lay one strip of pasta down on a flat board and place small teaspoonfuls of filling along the pasta in rows 4cm apart. Cover with another sheet of pasta, pressing down to avoid forming air pockets. Use a fluted pastry wheel or knife to cut between the rows to form small squares with filling in the centre of each. If the edges do not stick well, moisten with milk or water and press together with a fork.

Allow the ravioli to dry for 30 minutes on a board sprinkled with a little semolina flour before cooking. Turn occasionally so they dry on both sides.

FETTUCCINE BOLOGNESE

NOODLES WITH MEAT SAUCE

SERVES 4-6 / PREP: 20 MINUTES / COOK: 1 HOUR 30 MINUTES

Try a new twist on an old favourite by using ribbon pasta for this recipe. We think it makes for a heartier, meatier dish as the fettucine hold the Bolognese sauce better, and our customers agree. You can choose between fettuccine made with or without eggs. If you want to, prepare your sauce a day or two ahead and keep it in the fridge.

1 batch of Bolognese Sauce (see page 181)

500g De Cecco non-egg fettuccine, or 900g fresh egg fettuccine

a few sprigs of fresh flat-leaf parsley, finely chopped

salt

Bring a large pan of salted water to a rapid boil for the pasta.

Slowly bring the Bolognese sauce to simmering point in a large saucepan.

Drop the fettuccine into the boiling water and cook according to packet instructions (remember that egg pasta will cook faster than non-egg pasta).

Drain the pasta. Mix the fettuccine and the Bolognese sauce together and cook gently for a further minute. Divide between heated bowls and serve immediately, garnishing each plate with a sprinkling of parsley.

RAVIOLI DI SPINACI E RICOTTA

SPINACH AND RICOTTA RAVIOLI
SERVES 4 / PREP: 1 HOUR / COOK: 15 MINUTES

Spinach and ricotta is a classic filling for ravioli. Our version jazzes it up with marjoram and nutmeg. We pair these ravioli with a spring sauce of peas and crème fraîche. For 4 people we use fresh pasta made with 3 large eggs, 250g flour and 50g semolina flour (see page 72).

FILLING:

45ml ASK Italian extra virgin olive oil

100g baby spinach

180g ricotta

80g Parmesan or Grana Padano cheese, finely grated

a pinch of dried ground marjoram

a pinch of dried wild oregano

a pinch of freshly ground nutmeg

30g soft white breadcrumbs

freshly ground sea salt and black pepper

SAUCE:

30g unsalted butter

115g garden peas

12 fresh basil leaves, finely chopped

60ml (4 tablespoons) dry white wine

230g crème fraîche

100ml hot pasta cooking water

freshly grated nutmeg

60g baby spinach leaves

freshly ground sea salt and black pepper

First make the filling. This makes approximately 400g, for about 40 ravioli. Heat 1 tablespoon of the oil in a saucepan over a low heat. Add the spinach leaves and wilt slowly, stirring, for 2–3 minutes. Season lightly with salt and pepper. Allow to cool before chopping finely.

In a large bowl, combine the chopped spinach, ricotta, Parmesan or Grana Padano, and remaining extra virgin olive oil. Stir in the marjoram, oregano and nutmeg. Mix well. Taste for seasoning, adding salt and pepper as needed. Add the breadcrumbs, stirring to combine all the ingredients. The filling will keep for 1 day in the fridge if you want to make it in advance.

Make the pasta and fill the ravioli as instructed on pages 72-74. Bring a large pan of salted water to the boil for the pasta.

To make the sauce, melt the butter in a large saucepan. Add the peas and chopped basil and cook for a minute over a low heat. Stir in the wine, turn up the heat and cook until the wine has evaporated. Add the crème fraîche and the hot pasta cooking water, mixing well. Season with salt, pepper and nutmeg to taste.

Lower the heat, add the baby spinach and cook gently until it wilts. When you have added the spinach to the sauce, drop the ravioli into the pan of boiling water for 3–4 minutes. Remove from the water using a slotted spoon and delicately stir the ravioli into the pea sauce. Cook for 1–2 minutes more. Divide the ravioli between warmed serving bowls, spooning over any extra sauce.

RAVIOLI MARITTIMI

SEAFOOD RAVIOLI

SERVES 6 / PREP: 1 HOUR / COOK: 20 MINUTES

Here's a really classy ravioli recipe, combining delicate seafood in the filling with a light tomato and prawn sauce enriched with a touch of cream. For 6 people we use fresh pasta made with 4 large eggs, 325g flour and 75g semolina flour (see page 72).

FILLING:

200g ricotta

75g cooked salmon, flaked

70g crayfish tails, finely chopped

30g crabmeat

40ml double cream

1 tablespoon lemon juice

1 teaspoon finely chopped fresh dill

1 tablespoon fish stock or water

35g soft white breadcrumbs

freshly ground sea salt and black pepper

SAUCE:

3 tablespoons ASK Italian extra virgin olive oil

3 garlic cloves, finely chopped

85g (36) small cooked cold-water prawns

20 fresh basil leaves, finely chopped

350g tomato passata

175ml single cream

150ml hot pasta cooking water

2 tablespoons finely chopped fresh flat-leaf parsley

6 baby plum tomatoes, de-seeded and quartered

freshly ground sea salt and black pepper

First make the filling. This makes approximately 450g, for about 60 ravioli. In a large bowl, combine the ricotta, salmon, crayfish, crab, cream, lemon juice, dill and fish stock or water. Mix well. Taste and season with salt and pepper as necessary. Stir in the breadcrumbs and mix well. Now the mix is ready to fill the ravioli. The filling will keep in the fridge for 1 day, so you can prepare it in advance.

Make the pasta and fill the ravioli as instructed on pages 72-74. Bring a large pan of salted water to the boil for the pasta.

To make the sauce, heat the oil in a saucepan over a low heat. Add the garlic and sauté for 1–2 minutes, taking care not to let it brown. Stir in the prawns, basil, passata, cream, hot pasta cooking water and parsley. Bring the sauce gently to the boil and season to taste. Simmer over a low heat for 10 minutes, stirring occasionally.

When you are finishing the sauce, drop the ravioli into the pan of boiling water for 3–4 minutes. Remove from the water using a slotted spoon and delicately stir the ravioli into the tomato sauce. Cook for a further 1–2 minutes. Divide the ravioli between warmed serving bowls, spooning over any extra sauce. Garnish each portion with 4 tomato quarters.

FETTUCCINE CON VERDURE

NOODLES WITH VEGETABLES
SERVES 4-6 / PREP: 20 MINUTES / COOK: 15 MINUTES

Fettuccine, or 'little ribbons', are traditional egg noodles from the Roman area. Use either fresh or dried egg fettuccine, or dried durum wheat noodles as we do in the restaurants. Fiona Killala, our General Manager at Southend, says: 'This is a lovely spring pasta dish made with healthy seasonal vegetables, and it's a nice change that there's no creamy sauce.'

70g green beans, topped, tailed and cut in half

3 tablespoons ASK Italian extra virgin olive oil

1 garlic clove, finely chopped

240g (2 medium) courgettes cut into 1cm batons

220g peas

100g sun-dried tomatoes in oil, drained and cut into large pieces

80g baby spinach

10g (1 medium) red chilli, de-seeded and cut into rings

120ml water

20g (about 25) fresh basil leaves, finely chopped

500g De Cecco non-egg fettuccine, or 900g fresh egg fettuccine

80g Black Olive Tapenade (see page 45)

freshly ground sea salt and black pepper

Blanch the green beans by dropping them into rapidly boiling water for 2 minutes. Drain, refresh under cold water and set aside.

Heat 1 tablespoon of the oil in a saucepan over a low heat. Add the spinach leaves and wilt slowly, stirring, for 2-3 minutes. Season lightly with salt and pepper and set aside. Bring a large pan of salted water to the rolling boil for the pasta.

Heat the remainder of the oil in a large frying pan over a low heat. Add the chopped garlic and sauté lightly. Don't let it burn.

Add the courgettes and sauté gently for 3–4 minutes until they start to soften. Stir in the peas, sun-dried tomatoes, spinach, green beans, chilli and water and cook over a medium heat for a further 4 minutes. Stir in the basil and season with salt and pepper to taste. Keep warm while the pasta cooks.

Drop the fettuccine into the boiling water and cook according to packet instructions (remember that egg pasta will cook faster than non-egg pasta). Using a mug, scoop out a cupful of the pasta cooking water and set aside.

Drain the fettuccine and turn them into the pan with the sauce. Cook together over a medium heat for 2-3 minutes, stirring to blend the sauce with the noodles. If the sauce seems dry, add a little of the reserved pasta cooking water.

Divide the pasta into hot bowls and place a spoonful of tapenade on top of each dish. Serve immediately.

LASAGNE

SERVES 8 - 10 / PREP: 2 HOURS, IF YOU ARE MAKING PASTA FROM SCRATCH / COOK: 25 MINUTES

Every Italian family has its own version of lasagne. ASK Italian's is made with 4 layers of egg pasta layered with béchamel and Bolognese sauce and seasoned with Grana Padano. Prepare the sauces before making the pasta. You can substitute store-bought fresh pasta sheets for the home-made if you wish. Make the pasta on the day you are assembling the lasagne; the sauces can be made the day before. The pasta must be boiled briefly before the lasagne can be assembled.

1 batch of fresh lasagne made from 3 large eggs, 250g flour and 50g semolina flour (see page 72)

2 batches of Bolognese Sauce (see page 181)

1 batch of Béchamel Sauce (see page 181)

120g Parmesan or Grana Padano cheese, grated

40g butter

salt

Bring a large pan of salted water to the boil for the pasta. You'll need some clean tea cloths and a large flat surface to work on. Drop the lengths of pasta into the boiling water a few pieces at a time. Spread your tea cloths out on the tabletop. After the pasta pieces have cooked for just 1–2 minutes, carefully scoop them out with a slotted spoon and arrange them on a tea cloth. Don't overlap them or they will stick. Continue boiling in small batches until all the pasta has been cooked.

Preheat the oven to 200°C/400°F/gas mark 6.

Spread a little of the fat from the top of the Bolognese sauce around the bottom of the lasagne baking dish, about 32cm x 25cm x 6cm. Spoon a little of the Bolognese sauce in the bottom. Add a thin layer of béchamel, sprinkle with a bit of the grated cheese and cover with a layer of pasta. Try to make an even layer of pasta that goes right to the edge of the dish, but not up the sides. Repeat the sequence, with thin layers of Bolognese sauce, béchamel and cheese. You should use about one-third of the Bolognese sauce and one-fifth of the béchamel in each layer. Don't make the layers too thick: you just want the meat to be dotted through the béchamel. You should have enough for about 4 layers of each. Cover the final pasta sheets with a thin layer of béchamel and a sprinkling of cheese. Dot the top with butter.

Bake for 20–25 minutes or until the top is lightly browned. Let the lasagne rest for 5 minutes out of the oven before cutting into sections and serving alone or with a mixed salad.

Adrian recommends: ASK Italian's Chianti.

Rich pasta, with an intense meaty tomato sauce and light béchamel. Look no further than our own Chianti with its crisp, refreshing acidity, ripe cherry fruit and rich taste. It's the perfect match for our Bolognese-based lasagne.

LASAGNE DI CAPRINO, SPINACI E FUNGHI

GOAT'S CHEESE, SPINACH AND MUSHROOM LASAGNE

SERVES 8-10 / PREP: 2 HOURS, IF YOU ARE MAKING PASTA FROM SCRATCH / COOK: 25 MINUTES

This lovely lasagne was created by Pawel Skrobacz, our Head Chef at ASK Italian in Ipswich. Pawel won the Primo Pasta Chef of the Year competition in 2011, a contest we run every year for our Head Chefs. His prizes were an inspiring food trip to Italy, the chance to cook with Theo at the Theo Randall Restaurant in Mayfair, and the placing of his dish on ASK Italian's set menu. This lasagne has 4 layers.

---

1 batch of lasagne pasta (made from 3 large eggs, 250g flour and 50g semolina flour (see page 72)

1 batch of Béchamel Sauce made with 120g soft goat's cheese added after the milk (see page 181)

1 batch of Sautéed Mushrooms (see page 183)

230g cooked spinach (made from 250g fresh spinach leaves)

200g soft goat's cheese

½ teaspoon grated nutmeg

40g butter

salt and freshly ground black pepper

Follow the instructions for making and boiling pasta sheets for lasagne on page 72.

Preheat the oven to 200°C/400°F/gas mark 6.

Butter a lasagne baking dish, about 32cm x 25cm x 6cm. Spoon a little béchamel on the bottom of the dish and sprinkle with a few mushrooms. Cover with a layer of pasta. Try to make an even layer of pasta that goes right to the edge of the dish, but not up the sides. Spread the pasta with a layer of béchamel and around one-third each of the mushrooms and spinach. Dot with goat's cheese and sprinkle lightly with grated nutmeg. Season to taste. Cover with another layer of pasta. Repeat the sequence with 2 more layers. Cover the final pasta sheets with a thin layer of béchamel and the remaining goat's cheese. Dot the top with butter.

Bake for 20–25 minutes or until the top is lightly browned. Let the lasagne rest for 5 minutes before cutting into sections and serving alone or with a mixed salad.

CHAPTER 3
PRIMI: RISOTTO, FARRO AND POTATOES

When Italian first courses are not pasta based they're made of rice, grains or potatoes. You'll find delicious recipes for risotti, spelt wheat and gnocchi to serve as first or main courses.

HOW TO MAKE A PERFECT RISOTTO

Risotto is one of Italy's great contributions to gastronomy. How a simple batch of rice can be transformed – with just a few humble ingredients and some patient stirring – into a creamy, richly textured dish never ceases to amaze. It's not hard to make a risotto, you just need two things: the right kind of rice and the right method. That, and a strong arm. The rest is child's play.

THE RICE:

It's always best to use Italian medium-grain risotto rice, such as Arborio, Carnaroli, Baldo, Roma or the smaller Vialone Nano. These varieties have thick grains able to hold their shape and texture during cooking. Risotto won't work with delicate basmati, jasmine or pre-cooked rices. The ideal risotto should be a loose creamy mass in which the shape and texture of each individual grain can be felt and tasted. Not too wet, not too dry. The rice, like Italian pasta, is cooked al dente, just enough to soften it without losing its bite. As it is stirred, risotto rice releases its starches into a 'cream' that makes it so unique.

THE METHOD:

Whichever flavourings you choose, the basic technique for making risotto is the same. It's not hard to do but it requires 30 patient minutes: you can't walk away from a risotto once you've started it. You have to keep slowly stirring to stop the rice sticking to the pan and to activate those starches. Our recipes are designed to take you through the whole process, so just follow them and you'll be the creator of a great risotto!

You'll need a large, heavy-bottomed saucepan and a wooden spoon, so the equipment couldn't be simpler. The rice grains are first 'toasted' in hot oil, then wine is added and cooked until it evaporates, and only then is the main stock or liquid added, one ladleful at a time, while the rice is stirred until the grains have absorbed all the liquid and swollen very gradually. Flavourings and other ingredients are added in stages along the way. Risotto thickens as it cools so it's best eaten as soon as it's made. It can be reheated the following day, but the texture will be more solid.

RISOTTO AT ASK ITALIAN RESTAURANTS

We've introduced risotto onto our menus because we think it's so delicious and so authentically Italian. We've developed a way to make this family dish in a busy restaurant kitchen where we don't have the luxury of 30 minutes of stirring, instead adding a bit of cream to help us maintain the right texture. At home, you won't need to – unless you want to give our version a try.

After the onions are softened, the rice is 'toasted'

RISOTTO VERDE

GREEN VEGETABLE RISOTTO

SERVES 4-5 / PREP: 10 MINUTES / COOK: 45 MINUTES

Risotto Verde is a great vegetarian risotto which is chunky and rustic with lots of lovely green vegetables. You can adapt it by using your favourite vegetables and whatever's in season.

80g green beans, topped, tailed and halved

160g artichoke hearts, fresh, tinned in water or frozen

240g courgettes

3 tablespoons ASK Italian extra virgin olive oil

240g garden peas

1 tablespoon chopped fresh thyme

80g baby spinach

1.5 litres Vegetable Stock (see page 180)

100g butter

55g white onion, finely chopped

350g risotto rice, such as Arborio or Carnaroli

75ml white wine

20 fresh basil leaves, finely chopped, plus extra to garnish

50g Parmesan or Grana Padano cheese, grated

40g Fontal or Gruyère cheese, diced

freshly ground sea salt and black pepper

First prepare the vegetables: blanch the beans in a small pan of boiling water for 2 minutes, drain, cool under running water and set aside. Quarter the artichoke hearts. Cut the courgettes first into 1cm rings, then in half.

In a medium frying pan, heat 2 tablespoons of the oil and add the courgettes, cooking for 2–3 minutes until they start to soften. Stir in the artichokes, peas, blanched green beans, thyme and spinach. Cook for a further 2–3 minutes, or until the spinach leaves have wilted. Season lightly and set aside.

Bring the vegetable stock to a simmer on the back of the stove. Keep it hot while you make the risotto.

Heat 70g of the butter with 1 tablespoon of oil in a large heavy saucepan. Stir in the onion and cook over a low heat until it softens. Now pour in the rice and cook over a medium heat for 2–3 minutes, stirring constantly to 'toast' the rice and coat it with oil.

Pour in the wine, turn up the heat to medium and cook, stirring, until the liquid evaporates. Stir in one ladleful of hot vegetable stock, and cook until the liquid is absorbed. Keep stirring to prevent the rice from sticking to the pan.

Add a little more stock and stir again until the liquid is absorbed. Continue stirring and adding the liquid a ladleful at a time. After about 15 minutes of cooking time, stir in the vegetables. Taste the rice, seasoning with salt and pepper as needed. If you run out of hot stock, use hot water from the kettle, but don't worry if the rice is done before you have used all the stock. Each batch of rice is different.

Continue cooking, stirring and adding the liquid until the rice is al dente, or tender but still firm to the bite. The total cooking time of the risotto may vary from 20 to 35 minutes. When it is ready, remove it from the heat and beat in the basil, the remaining butter and the cheeses. Serve in flat bowls, garnished with a sprig of basil.

RISOTTO CON FUNGHI E PANCETTA

RISOTTO WITH MUSHROOMS AND PANCETTA
SERVES 4-5 / PREP: 10 MINUTES / COOK: 45 MINUTES

This autumnal risotto has featured on our autumn Specials menu. We garnish it with a slice of Speck, the smoked ham from northern Italy.

200g pancetta lardons

1 batch of Sautéed Mushrooms (see page 183)

1 teaspoon chopped fresh thyme

2 garlic cloves, finely chopped

1.5 litres chicken stock

100g butter

3 tablespoons ASK Italian extra virgin olive oil

55g white onion, finely chopped

350g risotto rice, such as Arborio or Carnaroli

75ml white wine

40g Grana Padano cheese, finely grated

4 slices Speck or Parma ham, cut into 4

freshly ground sea salt and black pepper

Sauté the pancetta in a medium frying pan over a low heat until the pork begins to render its fat and become crispy. Stir in the sautéed mushrooms, thyme and garlic and cook for 1–2 minutes. Set aside.

Bring the chicken stock to a simmer on the back of the stove. Keep it hot while you make the risotto.

Heat 70g of the butter with 1 tablespoon of olive oil in a large heavy saucepan. Stir in the onion and cook over a low heat until it softens. Now pour in the rice and cook over a medium heat for 2–3 minutes, stirring constantly to 'toast' the rice and coat it with the oil.

Pour in the wine, turn up the heat to medium and cook, stirring, until the liquid evaporates. Stir in one ladleful of hot chicken stock, and cook until the liquid is absorbed. Keep stirring to prevent the rice from sticking to the pan. Add a little more stock and stir again until the liquid is absorbed.

Stir in the pancetta and mushroom mixture. Continue adding the liquid a ladleful at a time and stirring until the liquid is absorbed. After about 15 minutes of cooking time, taste the rice, seasoning with salt and pepper as needed. If you run out of hot stock, use hot water from the kettle.

Continue cooking, stirring and adding the liquid until the rice is al dente, or tender but still firm to the bite. The total cooking time of the risotto may vary from 20 to 35 minutes. When it is ready, remove it from the heat and beat in the remaining butter and the cheese. Serve in flat bowls, garnished with pieces of Speck and a drizzling of extra virgin olive oil.

RISOTTO CON POLLO E FUNGHI

RISOTTO WITH CHICKEN AND MUSHROOMS

SERVES 4-5 / PREP: 10 MINUTES / COOK: 45 MINUTES

This risotto was the first to be introduced on the ASK Italian menu and is always very popular with our customers. We serve it with a little cream for extra richness. Add some at home at the end of cooking if you like that super-creamy texture.

3 tablespoons ASK Italian extra virgin olive oil

400g raw chicken breast, cut into thin strips

1 tablespoon chopped fresh tarragon or thyme

1 batch of Sautéed Mushrooms (see page 183)

500ml mushroom stock

1 litre chicken stock

100g butter

55g white onion, finely chopped

350g risotto rice, such as Arborio or Carnaroli

75ml white wine

4 tablespoons Grana Padano cheese, finely grated

freshly ground sea salt and black pepper

4 sprigs of fresh tarragon or thyme, to garnish

Heat 2 tablespoons of the oil in a small frying pan and brown the chicken lightly on all sides. Don't worry if the chicken is not cooked through. Stir in the herbs and the sautéed mushrooms, cooking for 1–2 minutes. Turn the chicken and mushrooms into a bowl and deglaze the pan with 3 tablespoons of water or stock, scraping up the cooking juices with a wooden spoon. Add them to the chicken.

Combine the stocks and bring to a simmer on the back of the stove. Keep the stock hot while you make the risotto.

Heat 70g of the butter with 1 tablespoon of olive oil in a large heavy saucepan. Stir in the onion and cook over a low heat until it softens. Now pour in the rice and cook over a medium heat for 2–3 minutes, stirring constantly to 'toast' the rice and coat it with the oil.

Pour in the wine, turn up the heat to medium and cook, stirring, until the liquid evaporates. Stir in one ladleful of hot stock, and cook until the liquid is absorbed. Keep stirring to prevent the rice from sticking to the pan. Add a little more stock and stir again until the liquid is absorbed.

Stir in the chicken and mushroom mixture. Add another ladleful of stock and stir again until the liquid is absorbed. Continue adding the liquid a ladleful at a time, stirring until the liquid is absorbed. After about 15 minutes of cooking time, taste the rice, seasoning with salt and pepper as needed.

Continue cooking, stirring and adding the liquid until the rice is al dente, or tender but still firm to the bite. The total cooking time may vary from 20 to 35 minutes. When it is ready, remove it from the heat and beat in the remaining butter and the cheese. Serve in flat bowls, garnished with a sprig of herbs.

Adrian recommends: ASK Italian's Nebbiolo or a Barolo DOCG 2007 like GD Vajra's 'Le Albe'.

The creamy risotto rice and earthy mushrooms give richness and complexity to this dish so we need a wine with good acidity, maturity, and complex fruit flavours showcasing earthiness and spice. Try a mature Barolo or our own wonderful Nebbiolo.

RISOTTO CON GAMBERONI E ZUCCHINE

RISOTTO WITH PRAWNS AND COURGETTES
SERVES 4-5 / PREP: 10 MINUTES / COOK: 45 MINUTES

Risotto is often paired with seafood and vegetables in summer. At ASK Italian we serve this risotto with chilli, cream and cheese in it. If you want it particularly creamy too, add a little cream at the end of the cooking. Use shell-on raw prawns, fresh or frozen.

325g raw king prawns in their shells

1.5 litres water

1 bay leaf

2 sprigs of fresh parsley

a few black peppercorns

2 garlic cloves, peeled

240g courgettes, cut into 1cm batons

2 tablespoons ASK Italian extra virgin olive oil

100g butter

55g white onion, finely chopped

350g risotto rice, such as Arborio or Carnaroli

75ml white wine

115g tomato passata, at room temperature

20g red chilli, cut into thin rings (optional)

15g fresh basil leaves, finely chopped, plus extra to garnish

60g Parmesan or Grana Padano cheese, grated (optional)

freshly ground sea salt and black pepper

Make your stock by placing the prawns in a large saucepan with the water, herbs, peppercorns and garlic. Bring to the boil and cook for about 4 minutes. Remove the prawns with a slotted spoon, setting the prettiest 5 aside. When the others are cool enough to handle, peel and chop them in half, returning the shells to the saucepan. Boil the shells for another 10 minutes. Strain. Return the stock to a clean saucepan, and keep it simmering gently while the risotto is being made.

Sauté the courgette batons for 2–3 minutes in the oil in a large heavy saucepan. Using a slotted spoon, remove the courgettes and put in a side dish. Put 70g of the butter in the same saucepan. When it has melted, stir in the onion and cook over a low heat until it softens. Now pour in the rice and cook over a medium heat for 2–3 minutes, stirring constantly to 'toast' the rice and coat it with the oil.

Pour in the wine, turn up the heat to medium and cook, stirring, until the liquid evaporates. Stir in one ladleful of hot prawn stock, and cook until the liquid is absorbed. Keep stirring to prevent the rice from sticking to the pan.

Add the tomato passata and optional chilli with a little more stock and stir again until the liquid is absorbed. Stir in the shelled prawns. Continue stirring and adding the liquid a ladleful at a time. After about 20 minutes of cooking time, stir in the courgettes and basil. Taste the rice, seasoning with salt and pepper as needed. If you run out of the hot broth, use hot water from the kettle.

Continue cooking, stirring and adding the liquid until the rice is al dente, or tender but still firm to the bite. The total cooking time of the risotto may vary from 20 to 35 minutes. When it is ready, remove it from the heat and beat in the remaining butter and optional cheese. Serve in flat bowls, garnished with the reserved king prawns and a sprig of basil.

FARRO AL POMODORO

SPELT IN TOMATO SAUCE
SERVES 4-6 / PREP: 20 MINUTES / COOK: 1 HOUR

Martyn Rose is a chef trainer at ASK Italian. He's enthusiastic about all types of Italian food and loves eating in Italy. Martyn says: 'Italians love eating grains, and farro – emmer wheat or spelt – was known in ancient Rome. It was fed to Roman soldiers to give them energy for their long marches. Today it's considered a superfood thanks to its high vitamin content. In Britain, farro can be found in Italian shops and health food stores.'

8 tablespoons extra virgin olive oil

1 garlic clove, lightly crushed

1 x 400g tin Italian tomatoes

zest of 1 lemon

1 small red onion, finely chopped

300g farro (semi-pearled)

500ml Vegetable Stock (see page 180), warmed

50g Parmesan or Grana Padano, grated

a pinch of dried oregano

freshly ground sea salt and black pepper

Preheat the oven to 200°C/400°F/gas mark 6.

Heat 2 tablespoons of the oil in a medium saucepan over a low heat. Add the garlic clove and cook for 1 minute. Stir in the tomatoes and their juice, crushing them with a wooden spoon. Season with salt and cook for 20 minutes. Using a wooden spoon, push the tomato sauce through a sieve into a bowl or blitz with a hand blender.

Drizzle a large shallow baking dish with 2 tablespoons of oil. Sprinkle evenly with the lemon zest.

Heat 3 tablespoons of oil in a large saucepan. Add the onion and cook over a low heat for 5–6 minutes, or until the onion softens and becomes translucent. Stir in ½ teaspoon of salt. Pour the farro into the pan and stir over a low heat for 1–2 minutes, until the grains are lightly coated with oil. Pour in the tomato sauce and the vegetable stock, mixing well. Stir in half the grated cheese and taste for seasoning. Bring the mixture to a simmer.

Turn the farro mixture into the prepared baking dish. Cover with foil and bake for 45–50 minutes. Remove from the oven, sprinkle with the remaining cheese, the oregano and a drizzle of extra virgin olive oil before serving.

Martyn Rose

GNOCCHI ALL'ARRABBIATA

POTATO GNOCCHI WITH SPICY TOMATO SAUCE

SERVES 4 / PREP: 10 MINUTES / COOK: 15 MINUTES

The Italians have found lots of colourful ways to name their dishes. This spicy tomato sauce is 'the angry woman's', and we love how its fiery, peppery tomatoes complement the soft potato gnocchi. Taste a tiny bit of your chilli before adding it to the sauce and adjust the amount depending on how hot you want the sauce to be.

2 tablespoons ASK Italian extra virgin olive oil

1 clove garlic, finely chopped

115g tomato passata

400g tin chopped tomatoes

4 Peppadew peppers, quartered

1 tablespoon red chilli, de-seeded and finely chopped

a handful of fresh basil leaves, chopped, plus a few sprigs to garnish

500g De Cecco Gnocchi di Patate or other fresh gnocchi

salt and freshly ground black pepper

Bring a large pan of salted water to a rapid boil for the gnocchi.

Heat the oil in a large frying pan. Add the garlic and cook gently for 1 minute. Stir in the tomato passata, chopped tomatoes, peppers, chilli and chopped basil. Season with salt and pepper to taste. Bring the sauce to the boil, reduce the heat and simmer for 10 minutes.

Drop the gnocchi into the boiling water and cook according to packet instructions. Drain, turn the gnocchi into the pan with the sauce and cook together over a medium heat for 1–2 minutes, stirring constantly.

Serve in warmed pasta dishes, topped with sliced basil.

GATTÒ DI PATATE

MASHED POTATO PIE

SERVES 6 / PREP: 40 MINUTES / COOK: 45 MINUTES

Carla says: This Neapolitan bake is a 'gateau' of mashed potato with cheese, ham and mozzarella, and dates to the Napoleonic age. It's very easy to make and is loved by Italian families, from the bambini to the nonna.

800g large potatoes

100g butter

2 handfuls of breadcrumbs

375ml milk

80g Parmesan cheese, grated, plus extra to finish

a pinch of ground mace or nutmeg

3 large eggs

120g mozzarella, diced

80g sliced cooked ham, diced

salt and freshly ground black pepper

Boil the potatoes until soft. Peel when cool enough to handle, and pass the potatoes through a mouli or potato ricer into a large mixing bowl. Beat in 80g of the butter.

Preheat the oven to 200°C/400°F/gas mark 6.

Butter a deep, high-sided baking dish, 22cm in diameter. Sprinkle with a handful of breadcrumbs, turning the dish around slowly to allow the breadcrumbs to stick to the butter on all sides.

Pour the milk into the potato mixture and mix well. Stir in the grated Parmesan and mace or nutmeg. Drop the eggs into the mashed potatoes and mix well until smooth. Taste for seasoning, adding salt and pepper as needed.

Spread half the potato mixture in the bottom of the baking dish in an even layer. Cover with the mozzarella and ham in an even layer. Spread the remaining potato mixture over the filling, smoothing the top to flatten. Sprinkle with the remaining breadcrumbs and a light grating of Parmesan. Dot with butter and bake for 20 minutes, or until the top is nicely golden. Serve hot or warm.

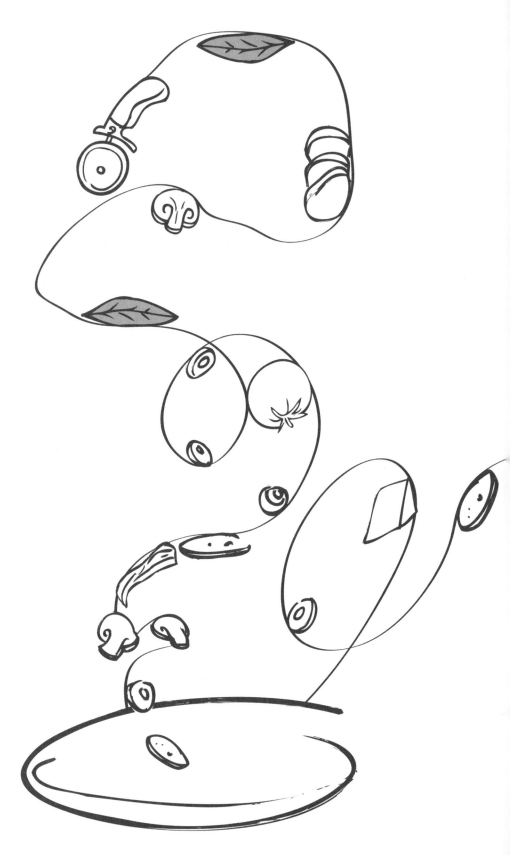

CHAPTER 4
PIZZA

ASK Italian loves pizza! It's one of our most popular dishes in the restaurants so we've included lots of ideas for pizza combinations to make at home from both our Classic and Prima Pizza ranges.

BASIC PIZZA DOUGH — HOW TO MAKE A PIZZA BASE

SERVES 4 / PREP: 1 HOUR 30 MINUTES / COOK: 20 MINUTES

Pizza dough is quick and easy to make and tastes much better than shop-bought pizza bases. Kids love making and eating pizza, so get them involved with choosing their favourite ingredients and making the pizzas ... they'll have a lot of fun. We have a range of kid's pizzas in the restaurants, but you can make them any way your kids fancy.

This recipe provides enough dough for 4 individual pizzas of around 30cm diameter each. This will serve 4 as a main course or 8 as an appetizer. If you divide the dough into 4 balls, each weighs around 170g.

If you don't want to use all the dough at once, you can freeze it once you have rolled it out and lined a pizza pan with it, before baking. Just thaw it and add your toppings before baking.

The recipe below explains how to make the dough. You can then just choose your favourite pizza from our recipes and use the toppings you like best, or make up your own combinations. Pizza is fun to make with kids too.

SERVES 4:

7g dried yeast (1 sachet easy-bake yeast)
or 25g fresh yeast cake

250ml water, lukewarm

1 teaspoon brown sugar

1 tablespoon extra virgin olive oil,
plus extra to oil the pan

1 teaspoon fine sea salt

450g strong white flour

In a small warmed bowl or jug, stir the yeast into the water, smoothing out the lumps with a fork. Stir in the sugar and oil. Allow to rest for a few minutes.

Meanwhile, sieve the salt and two-thirds (300g) of the flour into a large bowl. Make a well in the centre and stir in the yeast mixture gradually, mixing with a wooden spoon to form a ball as the dough starts to pull away from the sides of the bowl.

Dust a worktop with some of the remaining flour and knead the dough until smooth and elastic. Continue kneading for 8–10 minutes, working in the rest of the flour. The dough will be elastic and smooth. Wash and dry your hands.

Cut the dough into 4 equal pieces (170g each), and knead each piece into a smooth ball. Place the dough balls on a lightly floured tray with enough room for them to expand.

Cover with a damp tea cloth and place the tray in a warm, draught-free room. Let the dough rise for approximately 1 to 1½ hours or until the balls have doubled in size. The warmer the room, the faster they will rise.

TIP:
Using semolina flour to dust the work surface before kneading will give a crisper dough. That's how we make our pizzas at ASK Italian.

TIP:
Bake the dough within 10 minutes of forming it into circles.

TIP:
Make sure the oven is preheated and really hot when baking pizza. It should be at 240°C/475°F/gas mark 9. Turn it on at least 15 minutes before baking.

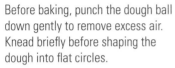

Before baking, punch the dough ball down gently to remove excess air. Knead briefly before shaping the dough into flat circles.

Pat the ball into a larger disc shape with your fingers, stretching the dough away from the centre.

Use a rolling pin to stretch the dough further. It should be about 5–7 mm thick. If you are using a circular pizza pan, roll the dough slightly larger than the pan to make the crust. Do not let the centre become too thin or the filling will seep through. The pizza should be 25–30cm in diameter.

Oil the pizza pan before placing the dough on it. If using a circular pan (circular pans with holes in them allow for a crisper, better cooked base), fit the dough into the pan, leaving the dough slightly thicker around the edge.

Our Prima Pizzas are made with the same quantity of dough per pizza, but stretched out longer into rectangles. The crust ends up a bit thinner and the pizzas can take more toppings. At home you can bake them as we do, by stretching them into rectangles about 30cm by 15cm, or bake them as normal in round pizza pans.

Spread the tomato sauce thinly using the back of a spoon.

Top with your favourite fillings (see our many recipes) and bake in the preheated oven for 15–20 minutes

We like to serve our pizzas with our home-made chilli oil on the side. You'll find the recipe on page 182.

TOMATO SAUCE FOR PIZZA

SERVES ENOUGH FOR 8 PIZZAS / PREP: 15 MINUTES / COOK: NONE

The tomato sauce we use as a base for our pizza toppings is produced specially for us in Italy by the Greci family. They grow the tomatoes from seed, harvest them and make our passata within 24 hours of picking. We have spent a long time working with them to ensure our recipe is authentic and unique. You can make your own version of our sauce by following the recipe below.

500g sieved tomato passata

a good pinch of dried wild oregano

5 fresh basil leaves, chopped

1 tablespoon ASK Italian extra virgin olive oil

freshly ground sea salt and black pepper

Mix all the ingredients in a bowl. Season with salt and pepper to taste. This will keep for 3 days in the refrigerator.

PIZZA MARGHERITA

PIZZA WITH MOZZARELLA, TOMATO AND BASIL

SERVES 4 AS A MAIN COURSE, 8 AS AN APPETIZER / PREP: 2 HOURS INCLUDING
DOUGH MAKING / COOK: 20 MINUTES

This is the mother of all pizzas, the simplest but best loved. It is named for the nineteenth-century Queen Margherita of Italy, whose favourite it was. This is Italy's most patriotic pizza, with the red, white and green ingredients symbolizing the Italian flag.

4 pizza dough bases on oiled trays or pizza pans (made from 1 Basic Pizza Dough Recipe, see page 106)

TOPPING:
240g (16 tablespoons) Tomato Sauce for Pizza (see above)

600g fresh mozzarella cheese, diced or grated

24 fresh basil leaves

a pinch of dried wild oregano

basil, to garnish

Preheat the oven to 240°C/475°F/gas mark 9. Turn it on at least 15 minutes before baking.

Spread the tomato sauce evenly over the pizza bases using the back of a spoon. Leave a little rim around the edges without sauce. Sprinkle evenly with the cheese. Dot with basil leaves and sprinkle with oregano.

Bake in the hot oven for around 15 minutes, or until the cheese is bubbling and the crust has browned. Garnish with more basil, cut and serve immediately.

Clockwise from top: Pizza Margherita, Pizza con Verdure, Pizza Fiorentina

PIZZA CON VERDURE

PIZZA WITH VEGETABLES

SERVES 4 AS A MAIN COURSE, 8 AS AN APPETIZER / PREP: 2 HOURS INCLUDING
DOUGH MAKING / COOK: 20 MINUTES

This is a colourful vegetarian pizza baked with artichokes, mushrooms and roasted red peppers and dressed with fresh rocket. You can substitute any of your favourite vegetables when they're in season.

4 pizza dough bases on oiled trays or pizza pans (made
from 1 Basic Pizza Dough recipe, see page 106)

TOPPING:

240g (16 tablespoons) Tomato Sauce for Pizza
(see previous page)

450g fresh mozzarella cheese, diced or grated

100g button mushrooms, thinly sliced

180g roasted red or yellow peppers, sliced

8 artichoke hearts in oil or brine, drained and quartered

24 black olives, pitted

40g Fontal or Gruyère cheese, cut into 5mm dice

4 handfuls of rocket leaves

4 tablespoons ASK Italian extra virgin olive oil

dried wild oregano

salt and freshly ground black pepper

Preheat the oven to 240°C/475°F/gas mark 9. Turn it on at least 15 minutes before baking.

Spread the tomato sauce evenly over the pizza bases using the back of a spoon. Leave a little rim around the edges without sauce. Sprinkle evenly with the mozzarella. Season lightly with salt and pepper. Distribute the vegetables, olives and Fontal or Gruyère cheese evenly between the pizzas and sprinkle with the oregano.

Bake in the hot oven for 15 minutes or until the cheese is bubbling and the crust has browned.

While the pizza is cooking, toss the rocket with the olive oil. Just before serving, garnish the centre of the hot pizzas with the rocket leaves.

PIZZA FIORENTINA

PIZZA WITH SPINACH AND EGG

SERVES 2 / PREP: 2 HOURS INCLUDING DOUGH MAKING / COOK: 20 MINUTES

The Florentines have been given credit for this appealing combination of spinach, cheese and egg. It's one of our most popular meatless dishes, and easy to make at home.

2 pizza dough bases on an oiled tray or in 30cm pans (made from half of the Basic Pizza Dough recipe, see page 106)

TOPPING:

120g (8 tablespoons) Tomato Sauce for Pizza (see page 111)

230g mozzarella cheese, diced or grated

100g cooked spinach (made from 130g raw spinach)

20 pitted black olives

20g Fontal or Gruyère cheese, diced

2 large eggs

Parmesan cheese, for grating

a pinch of dried wild oregano

Preheat the oven to 240°C/475°F/gas mark 9. Turn it on at least 15 minutes before baking.

Spread the tomato sauce evenly over the pizza bases using the back of a spoon. Leave a little rim around the edges without sauce. Sprinkle evenly with the mozzarella. Divide the spinach, olives and Fontal cheese between the pizzas and scatter evenly on top.

Bake in the hot oven for 8 minutes. Remove from the oven and carefully break one egg onto the middle of each pizza, taking care not to break the yolks.

Return to the oven and continue baking for 6–8 minutes, or until the cheese is bubbling and the crust has browned. If you prefer your egg runny, take the pizza out sooner.

Remove from the oven. Grate a little Parmesan on top and sprinkle with oregano. Serve immediately.

PIZZA CON POLLO PICCANTE E PANCETTA

PIZZA WITH SPICY CHICKEN AND PANCETTA

SERVES 2 AS A MAIN COURSE, 4 AS AN APPETIZER / PREP: 2 HOURS INCLUDING
DOUGH MAKING / COOK: 20 MINUTES

The chicken cooks on top of the pizza in this hearty all-in-one dish. Serve it with a crisp side salad.

2 pizza dough bases on an oiled tray or in 30cm pans (made from half of the Basic Pizza Dough recipe, see page 106)

TOPPING:

120g (8 tablespoons) Tomato Sauce for Pizza (see page 111)

200g chicken breast, sliced thinly

40g pancetta, diced

50g button mushrooms, sliced thinly

10 thin slices fresh chilli, or to taste

90g roasted red peppers, sliced

230g fresh mozzarella cheese, diced or grated

20g Fontal or Gruyère cheese, in 5mm dice

1 tablespoon finely chopped fresh parsley

2 pinches of dried wild oregano

Preheat the oven to 240°C/475°F/gas mark 9. Turn it on at least 15 minutes before baking.

Spread the tomato sauce evenly over the pizza bases using the back of a spoon. Leave a little rim around the edges without sauce. Top the pizza with the chicken, pancetta, mushrooms, chilli and peppers. Distribute the mozzarella and the Fontal or Gruyère evenly over the pizzas.

Bake in the hot oven for 15 minutes or until the cheese is bubbling and the crust has browned. Sprinkle with the herbs before cutting and serving.

PIZZA STROMBOLI

PIZZA WITH PEPPERONI SAUSAGE

SERVES 2 AS A MAIN COURSE, 4 AS AN APPETIZER / PREP: 2 HOURS INCLUDING
DOUGH MAKING / COOK: 20 MINUTES

Stromboli is a small volcanic island off the northern coast of Sicily. The inhabitants are used to the volcano's moods, as it huffs and puffs quite often. Sometimes there are even bursts of fiery explosions, like the spicy sausage in this pizza.

2 pizza dough bases on an oiled tray or in 30cm pans (made from half of the Basic Pizza Dough recipe, see page 106)

TOPPING:

120g (8 tablespoons) Tomato Sauce for Pizza (see page 111)

70g (60 small discs) pepperoni sausage

230g fresh mozzarella cheese, diced or grated

a pinch of dried wild oregano

Preheat the oven to 240°C/475°F/gas mark 9. Turn it on at least 15 minutes before baking.

Spread the tomato sauce evenly over the pizza bases using the back of a spoon. Leave a little rim around the edges without sauce. Distribute the pepperoni slices around the pizzas. Sprinkle evenly with the cheese.

Bake in the hot oven for around 15 minutes, or until the cheese is bubbling and the crust has browned. Sprinkle with the oregano, cut and serve immediately.

PRIMA PIZZA CAPRINA

PRIMA PIZZA WITH GOAT'S CHEESE

SERVES 4 AS A MAIN COURSE, 8 AS AN APPETIZER / PREP: 2 HOURS INCLUDING
DOUGH MAKING / COOK: 20 MINUTES

*Our restaurant in Spice Quay in London sells the most Prima Pizzas in the country:
one in five main meals they sell is a Prima Pizza! This one takes a Margherita base
and dresses it after baking with creamy goat's cheese, black olive tapenade and a
rocket salad... simply scrumptious! We like to serve these pizzas with our home-
made chilli oil (see page 182).*

*4 pizza dough bases on oiled trays or pizza pans (made
from 1 Basic Pizza Dough recipe, see page 106)*

TOPPING:

*240g (16 tablespoons) Tomato Sauce for Pizza
(see page 111)*

450g fresh mozzarella cheese, diced

dried wild oregano

60g (4 handfuls) rocket leaves

4 tablespoons ASK Italian extra virgin olive oil

180g soft goat's cheese, crumbled or diced

12 baby plum tomatoes, sliced in thirds

60g (4 tablespoons) Black Olive Tapenade (see page 45)

freshly ground black pepper

Preheat the oven to 240°C/475°F/gas mark 9. Turn it on at
least 15 minutes before baking.

Spread the tomato sauce evenly over the pizza bases
using the back of a spoon. Leave a little rim around the
edges without sauce. Sprinkle evenly with the mozzarella
and oregano.

Bake in the hot oven for 15 minutes or until the cheese is
bubbling and the crust has browned. While the pizza is
baking, toss the rocket leaves with the olive oil and season
with black pepper.

After you've taken the pizzas out of the oven, top them
with the rocket, goat's cheese and fresh tomatoes.
Serve immediately.

PRIMA PIZZA PROSCIUTTO E BUFALA

PROSCIUTTO AND BUFFALO MOZZARELLA PRIMA PIZZA

SERVES 4 / PREP: 2 HOURS INCLUDING DOUGH MAKING / COOK: 20 MINUTES

Buffalo mozzarella is one of Italy's star ingredients, but as it's less elastic in the oven than mozzarella made from cow's milk, we add it after baking. We serve only top-quality Italian buffalo mozzarella from Campania in our restaurants. This recipe combines the best of both types.

4 pizza dough bases on oiled trays or pizza pans (made from 1 Basic Pizza Dough recipe, see page 106)

TOPPING:

240g (16 tablespoons) Tomato Sauce for Pizza (see page 111)

450g fresh cow's milk mozzarella cheese, diced

dried wild oregano

60g (4 handfuls) rocket leaves

4 tablespoons ASK Italian extra virgin olive oil

200g buffalo mozzarella, torn into small pieces

8 slices prosciutto, Parma ham or Speck, each cut into 4

freshly ground black pepper

Preheat the oven to 240°C/475°F/gas mark 9. Turn it on at least 15 minutes before baking.

Spread the tomato sauce evenly over the pizza bases using the back of a spoon. Leave a little rim around the edges without sauce. Sprinkle evenly with the cow's milk mozzarella and oregano.

Bake in the hot oven for 15 minutes or until the cheese is bubbling and the crust has browned. While the pizza is baking, toss the rocket leaves with the olive oil and season with black pepper.

After you've taken the pizzas out of the oven, top them with the rocket, buffalo mozzarella, prosciutto pieces, and serve.

PRIMA PIZZA QUATTRO STAGIONI

FOUR SEASONS PRIMA PIZZA

SERVES 4 / PREP: 2 HOURS INCLUDING DOUGH MAKING / COOK: 20 MINUTES

This Prima Pizza is divided into four sections, each representing one season. You can adapt it to include your favourite seasonal foods. Bake it as we do, in long rectangles, or make round pizzas in your baking trays.

4 pizza dough bases on oiled trays or pizza pans (made from 1 Basic Pizza Dough recipe, see page 106)

TOPPING:

240g (16 tablespoons) Tomato Sauce for Pizza (see page 111)

450g fresh mozzarella cheese, diced or grated

4 artichoke hearts, quartered

50g Fontal or Gruyère cheese, diced

100g cooked spinach (made from 130g fresh)

4 slices Speck or prosciutto, each cut into 4 pieces

4 tablespoons Balsamic Onions (see page 179)

1 roasted red pepper, sliced

4 teaspoons Lilliput or other small capers

4 anchovy fillets, sliced lengthways

100g button mushrooms, thinly sliced

Parmesan or Grana Padano cheese, grated

dried wild oregano

Preheat the oven to 240°C/475°F/gas mark 9. Turn it on at least 15 minutes before baking.

Spread the tomato sauce evenly over the pizza bases using the back of a spoon. Leave a little rim around the edges without sauce. Sprinkle evenly with the mozzarella.

Arrange the artichoke heart pieces on one quarter of each pizza and dot with Fontal cheese. Distribute the spinach and Speck on the second quarter of each pizza. Spread the balsamic onions, red pepper, capers and anchovies on the third quarters, and complete the pizzas by scattering the mushroom slices topped with grated Parmesan on the final quarters.

Bake in the hot oven for around 15 minutes, or until the cheese is bubbling and the crust has browned. Sprinkle a little oregano over the pizzas. Serve immediately, with chilli oil if you wish (see page 182).

PRIMA PIZZA CON FUNGHI E PANCETTA

PRIMA PIZZA WITH MUSHROOMS, PANCETTA AND CHEESE SAUCE

SERVES 4 AS A MAIN COURSE, 8 AS AN APPETIZER / PREP: 2 HOURS INCLUDING
DOUGH MAKING / COOK: 20 MINUTES

This special Prima Pizza is made 'in bianco', without tomato sauce, and has a deliciously creamy cheese sauce as a base instead. Have all the ingredients ready before you top and bake the pizzas. In the restaurants we like to serve this pizza with spicy chilli oil (see page 182).

4 pizza dough bases on oiled trays or pizza pans
(made from 1 Basic Pizza Dough recipe, see page 106)

TOPPING:

340g Cheese Sauce (see below)

440g Sautéed Mushrooms (see page 183)

100g cooked spinach (made from 130g raw spinach)

240g Balsamic Onions (see page 179)

160g pancetta, in small batons or cubes

8 tablespoons crème fraîche

4 tablespoons grated Parmesan or Grana Padano cheese

a pinch of dried wild oregano

Preheat the oven to 240°C/475°F/gas mark 9. Turn it on at least 15 minutes before baking.

Spread the cheese sauce evenly over the pizza bases using the back of a spoon. Leave a little rim around the edges without sauce. Divide the sautéed mushrooms, spinach and balsamic onions between the 4 pizzas, spreading the vegetables so they are evenly spaced. Top with the pancetta and small dollops of the crème fraîche.

Bake in the hot oven for 12–15 minutes or until the crust has browned. Remove from the oven, garnish with the grated Parmesan or Grana Padano and oregano, and serve immediately.

CHEESE SAUCE:

25g butter

25g flour

300ml milk

75g mature Cheddar cheese, grated

salt and freshly ground black pepper

Makes 340g, enough for 4 pizzas.

Melt the butter in a saucepan and whisk in the flour. Cook for 2 minutes over a low heat, stirring constantly. Add the milk in a slow, steady stream, stirring to prevent lumps. The sauce will thicken as it cooks. When the sauce has come to the boil, add the cheese and stir over a medium heat until it melts. Remove from the heat and season with salt and pepper.

PRIMA PIZZA CON GAMBERETTI E ZUCCHINE

PRIMA PIZZA WITH PRAWNS AND COURGETTES

SERVES 4 AS A MAIN COURSE, 8 AS AN APPETIZER / PREP: 2 HOURS INCLUDING DOUGH MAKING / COOK: 20 MINUTES

This cheese-less pizza is one of Theo's favourites. Our terrific pizza base is topped with seafood and vegetables, flavoured with Italian seasonings and given a special touch with crème fraîche.

4 pizza dough bases on oiled trays or pizza pans (made from 1 Basic Pizza Dough recipe, see page 106)

TOPPING:

240g (16 tablespoons) Tomato Sauce for Pizza (see page 111)

160g small cooked cold-water prawns

400g courgettes, finely sliced into long strips using a cheese grater with the slicer blade

4 tablespoons capers, drained

8 anchovy fillets, coarsely chopped

2 garlic cloves, finely chopped

8 tablespoons crème fraîche

dried wild oregano

freshly ground black pepper

lemon wedges, to garnish

Preheat the oven to 240°C/475°F/gas mark 9. Turn it on at least 15 minutes before baking.

Spread the tomato sauce evenly over the pizza bases using the back of a spoon. Leave a little rim around the edges without sauce. Season lightly with pepper.

Top evenly with the prawns, courgettes, capers, anchovy and garlic. Add the crème fraîche in small dollops. Sprinkle with oregano.

Bake in the hot oven for 15 minutes, or until the crust has browned. Cut the pizza into sections and serve with lemon wedges.

 Adrian recommends: ASK Italian's Gavi or a Gavi di Gavi DOCG 2011 such as La Scolca.

This light seafood pizza with delicate herbal flavours works well with a light, crisp, refreshing Gavi that won't overpower the food but has just enough depth and complexity to complement the dish.

CHAPTER 5
SECONDI: FISH AND MEAT

It's easy to turn a simple piece of fish or meat into an Italian delicacy by using aromatic flavourings like tomatoes and herbs. Our main course recipes go from sea bass and squid to chicken, beef, pork and lamb.

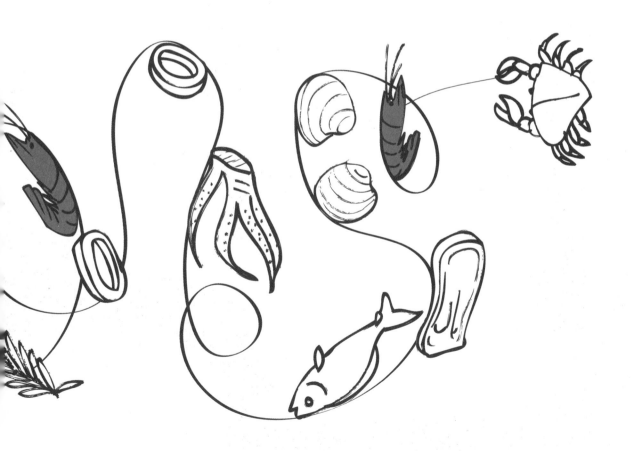

BRANZINO CON VERMOUTH E LIMONE

SEA BASS IN A LEMON, BASIL AND VERMOUTH SAUCE

SERVES 2 / PREP: 10 MINUTES / COOK: 25 MINUTES

Theo says: This is a super-simple recipe that is special enough to serve at a dinner party. Baking in foil retains all of the flavour of the fish and gives you the most amazing juice. All you need to do is add a bit of butter. Serve with rice or boiled new potatoes and steamed spinach.

75g unsalted butter

2 x 120g sea bass fillets, middle cut

½ a lemon, thinly sliced

a sprig of fresh thyme

4 leaves of basil (whole)

60ml vermouth

4 leaves of fresh basil

salt and freshly ground black pepper

Preheat the oven to 190°C/375°F/gas mark 5.

Fold 2 sheets of tin foil into large squares and butter the shiny sides. Place one bass fillet on each buttered square of foil, skin-side up. Top each portion with 2 slices of lemon, 3 thyme leaves, 25g of butter, salt and pepper.

Fold the foil over the fish to make an envelope, and pour 50ml of vermouth into each pocket. Leave for a few seconds to settle, and then crimp the envelope edges to seal. Place on a baking tray and bake in the oven for 15 minutes.

Once cooked, remove the fish from the oven and strain the juice from each parcel into a saucepan. Bring to the boil and reduce by half, add basil then whisk in the remaining butter.

Arrange each piece of fish with its lemon slices and basil on a warmed plate. Pour over the sauce and serve.

CALAMARI RIPIENI

STUFFED CALAMARI

SERVES 4 / PREP: 30 MINUTES / COOK: 45 MINUTES

Carla says: Tender calamari, or squid, have become much easier to find in the UK, so enjoying them is no longer confined to seaside suppers on the Mediterranean. They are simple to cook and can be stuffed with all sorts of fillings. If you buy the squid fresh, follow the instructions below for cleaning them.

700g fresh calamari

½ a lemon

3 medium tomatoes, peeled, seeded and finely chopped

2 anchovy fillets, chopped

1 tablespoon capers, roughly chopped

2 garlic cloves, finely chopped

75g plain breadcrumbs

4 tablespoons chopped fresh flat-leaf parsley, plus a few sprigs to garnish

1 large egg

3 tablespoons extra virgin olive oil

175ml dry white wine

salt and freshly ground black pepper

If your calamari have not been cleaned, take them to the sink and start by peeling the thin skin from the body section. Rinse. Pull the tentacles and head away from the body section, or sac. Some of the intestines will come away with the head. Remove and discard the translucent quill and any remaining insides from the sac. Cut the tentacles from the head. Discard the head and intestines. Remove and discard the small hard lump (beak) from the base of the tentacles. Place the tentacles in a bowl of water with the juice of half a lemon. Rinse the sacs well under cold running water. Pat the insides dry with paper towels.

Preheat the oven to 180°C/350°F/gas mark 4.

Combine the tomatoes, anchovies, capers, garlic, breadcrumbs and parsley in a small bowl. Stir in the egg. Season to taste. Drain and chop the tentacles coarsely. Add them to the breadcrumb mixture.

Stuff the calamari sacs loosely with the filling. Don't fill them too full as the calamari will shrink as they cook. Close the openings with toothpicks.

Grease a shallow baking dish large enough to hold the calamari in one layer. Arrange the calamari in the dish. Pour over the olive oil and wine. Bake, uncovered, for 35–45 minutes, or until tender. Remove the toothpicks before serving with rice.

POLLO CON PROSCIUTTO E MASCARPONE

CHICKEN WITH MASCARPONE AND PROSCIUTTO

SERVES 4 / PREP: 10 MINUTES / COOK: 20 MINUTES

Theo says: This easy but elegant recipe is perfect if you like the skin on your chicken crispy but the meat juicy. The prosciutto seasons the meat and the lemony mascarpone makes a great sauce. Look for organic chicken breasts with the skin left on.

2 sprigs of fresh thyme, leaves picked and chopped

zest and juice of 1½ lemons

150g mascarpone

4 organic chicken breasts, skin left on

4 slices prosciutto or Parma ham

2 tablespoons extra virgin olive oil

salt and freshly ground black pepper

Preheat the oven to 200°C/400°F/gas mark 6.

In a small bowl, stir the thyme, lemon zest and juice into the mascarpone.

Place the chicken on a chopping board, skin-side up. Gently pull the skin away from the breast to make a cavity, leaving it attached on the long side. Lay a piece of prosciutto onto the breast, under the skin, and spread a spoonful of the mascarpone mixture on top. Cover with the skin. Repeat with the other breasts.

Heat the oil in a heavy-based, ovenproof frying pan over a medium to high heat. Season the breasts with salt and pepper and place them, skin-side down, into the pan for 2 minutes or until the skin is golden.

Place the pan in the oven for 10–12 minutes, or until the breasts are pale pink but not raw in the centre. Remove the chicken from the pan. Drain any excess fat from the pan. The pan should have some lovely chicken juices and a few nuggets of cooked mascarpone. Stir in a tablespoon of mascarpone to bind the sauce.

Serve the chicken skin-side up on heated plates. Pour the pan juices over the chicken and serve with a fresh green vegetable.

TAGLIATA DI MANZO

SLICED STEAK WITH ROCKET AND TOMATOES

SERVES 4 / PREP: 10 MINUTES / COOK: 10 MINUTES

'La tagliata' is the Italian way to enjoy steak. You find it on all the best Italian trattoria menus, from north to south. Tagliare means to slice, but the way the Italians serve their sliced steak topped with a crisp layer of greens and reds and a drizzling of extra virgin olive oil makes this really unique. You can pan-fry the steak as we do here, or grill it on the barbecue. This has been a popular Special on the ASK Italian menu.

4 x 225g sirloin steaks

4 tablespoons ASK Italian extra virgin olive oil

60g rocket leaves

175g baby plum tomatoes, cut into thirds

freshly ground sea salt and black pepper

Salsa Verde (see page 182)

Rub the steaks with 2 tablespoons of the olive oil, salt and pepper, and leave them to marinate for 10 minutes.

Heat a large heavy frying pan until very hot. Place the steaks in the hot pan and cook for 2–3 minutes. Turn the steaks over and cook for a further 2–3 minutes for meat that is medium rare. Remove the steaks from the pan and place on a cutting board to rest.

Toss the rocket and tomatoes in a bowl with 2 tablespoons of olive oil, salt and pepper.

Slice the meat into 2cm slices, following the grain of the meat to obtain a juicier steak. Arrange the steak slices on a large warmed platter and scatter the rocket and tomatoes evenly over the meat. Serve with a bowl of salsa verde on the side.

SALTIMBOCCA

BEEF ROLLS WITH SAGE AND HAM

SERVES 4 / PREP: 15 MINUTES / COOK: 15 MINUTES

Carla says: Saltimbocca means 'to jump into your mouth', and these delicious and simple Roman beef rolls are so good they will! Use aromatic fresh sage leaves to make them, as they taste much better than dried sage.

8 small beef or veal escalopes
8 small slices prosciutto
8 fresh sage leaves
50g butter
100ml meat broth or stock, warmed
salt and freshly ground black pepper

Using a mallet or bottle, gently pound the beef slices until thin. Lay one slice of prosciutto over each escalope. Top with a sage leaf and season with salt and pepper. Roll the escalopes around the filling and secure each roll with a wooden toothpick.

Heat half the butter in a frying pan just large enough to hold the rolls in one layer. When it's bubbling, add the meat, turning the rolls to brown them on all sides. Cook for about 5–7 minutes. Transfer them to a warmed serving plate.

Add the remaining butter and the hot broth or stock to the frying pan. Bring to the boil, scraping up the brown residue on the bottom of the pan with a wooden spoon. Pour the sauce over the beef rolls, and serve.

MAIALE AL FORNO

PORK LOIN WRAPPED IN COPPA DI PARMA

SERVES 4 / PREP: 20 MINUTES / COOK: 40 MINUTES

Theo says: Coppa di Parma is a wonderful pork speciality from the area where they make the best prosciutto, Emilia Romagna. Coppa is salt-cured pork shoulder, whereas prosciutto is made from the animal's hind leg. Coppa is marbled with sweet fat, which keeps it moist during cooking. If you can't find Coppa, use prosciutto di Parma instead. Serve this dish with Potato, Fennel and Parmesan Gratin (see next page), which can be baked at the same time.

a sprig of fresh rosemary

30g unsalted butter, at room temperature

zest and juice of 1 lemon

1kg organic pork loin trimmed of skin and half of its fat

120g sliced Coppa di Parma

extra virgin olive oil

1 glass dessert wine (Recioto di Soave or Marsala)

salt and freshly ground black pepper

Preheat the oven to 190°C/375°F/gas mark 5.

Pick the rosemary leaves from their stalk and chop them. In a small bowl, stir the butter with a wooden spoon until smooth. Stir in the rosemary, lemon zest and lemon juice to form a paste. Spread the flavoured butter all over the pork loin. Season with salt and pepper.

On a flat surface, lay out a sheet of greaseproof paper. Lay the slices of Coppa di Parma over the paper in one layer that is a bit larger than the pork loin. Place the pork at one end of the Coppa and roll the paper around the loin so that the Coppa forms a second skin for it. Carefully remove the paper and tie the Coppa to the loin with string.

Heat a large ovenproof pan a bit larger than the loin and pour in a dash of olive oil. When the oil is hot, place the pork loin in the pan and seal it on one side for 2 minutes. Turn the meat over and put greaseproof paper on top. Bake in the oven for 30–40 minutes.

Remove the pan from the oven, and take the pork loin out to rest while you skim off the fat from the pan. Put the pan over a medium heat on the stove and deglaze the pan by pouring in the dessert wine and stirring the wine and pan juices together for 5 minutes. Return the meat to the pan and baste for at least 2 minutes. Serve sliced.

PATATE E FINOCCHI GRATINATI

POTATO, FENNEL AND PARMESAN GRATIN
SERVES 6 / PREP: 15 MINUTES / COOK: 35 MINUTES

1kg Roseval or other red-skinned potatoes

3 fennel bulbs

1 garlic clove, chopped

250ml double cream

300g Parmesan cheese, grated

salt and freshly ground black pepper

Preheat the oven to 190°C/375°F/gas mark 5.

Peel potatoes and cut into 1cm pieces. Slice the fennel into wedges 1cm thick. Blanch the potatoes in a pan of rapidly boiling water for 3-4 minutes. When they are cooked through, remove from the pan with a slotted spoon and blanch the fennel in the same water. Drain the vegetables, saving the cooking liquid to use in a soup or risotto.

Mix the garlic and cream into the potatoes and fennel. Stir in 200g of the Parmesan. Mix well and taste, adding salt and pepper if necessary. Turn the mixture into a ceramic baking dish. Cover with tin foil and bake in the oven for 15 minutes. Remove the foil, sprinkle with the remaining Parmesan and continue baking to brown the top for a further 15 minutes.

SPALLA D'AGNELLO CON OLIVE

SLOW-COOKED LAMB SHOULDER WITH ANCHOVIES, OLIVES AND ROSEMARY

SERVES 6 / PREP: 15 MINUTES / COOK: 2 HOURS

Theo says: This dish is ideal for Sunday lunch. Once it is in the oven, just leave it for 2 hours and enjoy the most tender and delicious lamb with the best Italian flavourings. Your butcher will bone the lamb shoulder for you. I like to serve this lamb with sprouting broccoli and potatoes.

1 lamb shoulder, boned

2 tablespoons extra virgin olive oil

6 garlic cloves, peeled

8 anchovy fillets

50g Taggiasche or other sweet, small black olives

a sprig of fresh rosemary

250ml white wine

Preheat the oven to 170°C/325°F/gas mark 3. Trim any excess fat from the lamb.

Heat the oil in a heavy casserole or ovenproof saucepan over a high heat. Seal the lamb, turning it to brown evenly. Turn off the heat, take the lamb out of the pan and spoon off any excess fat.

Put the garlic, anchovies, olives and rosemary in the pan. Pour in the wine. Place the meat back in the pan, and cover with foil. Bake for 2 hours.

While the lamb is resting out of the oven, prepare your vegetables. Serve with the sliced lamb.

Adrian recommends: a Chianti Classico DOCG 2007 such as Cecchi Riserva di Famiglia.

The lovely, delicate lamb flavours are enhanced by a combination of olives, anchovies and rosemary. Match with an aged Chianti that shows great elegance and similar savoury characters with just enough structure to complement rather than overpower the dish.

CHAPTER 6
CONTORNI: SALADS AND VEGETABLES

Contorni are Italian side dishes but we love using these colourful salads and vegetables as main courses too. You'll find several of ASK Italian's most popular salads here as well as ideas for turning green beans, peas or peppers into authentic Italian accompaniments.

INSALATA CAPRESE

TOMATO, MOZZARELLA AND BASIL SALAD
SERVES 4-6 / PREP: 10 MINUTES / COOK: NONE

This quintessentially Italian salad is always a favourite, especially in summer when tomatoes are sweet and plentiful. Use more than one variety of ripe tomato, such as Santos, San Marzano or other plum tomatoes. Serve it as a starter or main course.

225g vine-ripened tomatoes, sliced into 3 pieces

60g rocket leaves

20g fresh basil leaves, torn into large pieces

4–6 tablespoons ASK Italian extra virgin olive oil

200g buffalo mozzarella, torn into bite-size pieces

4 fresh basil leaves, finely chopped

freshly ground sea salt and black pepper

Mix the tomatoes, rocket and torn basil in a bowl. Drizzle with olive oil and season with salt to taste.

Arrange the salad on a platter. Top with the torn mozzarella, and drizzle with a little more oil and a grinding of black pepper. Garnish with the chopped basil and serve.

INSALATA DI RUCOLA

ROCKET SALAD
SERVES 4 / PREP: 10 MINUTES / COOK: NONE

This is a good side salad to accompany pizza or pasta. The peppery rocket complements the nutty flavours of the Grana Padano cheese. We use Fresh Olive Company Balsamic 5 vinegar, which is sold in all the ASK Italian restaurants. Try some!

80g rocket leaves

2 large ripe tomatoes, de-seeded and chopped into 1cm cubes.

6 tablespoons ASK Italian extra virgin olive oil

4 tablespoons balsamic vinegar

60g Grana Padano cheese

Put the rocket leaves and tomatoes in a bowl and toss with the olive oil and balsamic vinegar.

Divide the salad between small serving bowls, stacking the leaves high. Top with shavings of Grana Padano.

INSALATA DI FORMAGGIO DI CAPRA

GOAT'S CHEESE SALAD

SERVES 2 / PREP: 15 MINUTES / COOK: 5-10 MINUTES

Here's a delicious salad you can whip up for lunch. It features crostini topped with warmed goat's cheese, or caprino, and sun-dried tomatoes, served over a nicely complex salad that will hold your interest right to the last bite.

GOAT'S CHEESE CROSTINI:

4 x 1cm slices sourdough or Altamura bread

90g soft goat's cheese

6 sun-dried tomatoes in oil, drained and cut into large pieces

a pinch of dried wild oregano

SALAD:

100g Cos lettuce, sliced into strips

60g baby spinach

4 baby plum tomatoes, halved

8 cucumber slices

a handful of green beans, blanched for 2 minutes in boiling water

250g can butter beans, drained and rinsed

6 Peppadew peppers, quartered

4 tablespoons Balsamic Onions (see page 179)

120g Peeled Grilled Peppers, sliced into strips (see page 182)

120ml (8 tablespoons) Creamy Herb Dressing (see page 178)

Preheat the oven to 220°C/425°F/gas mark 7.

To make the crostini, spread the bread with the goat's cheese. Top with the sun-dried tomatoes and a pinch of oregano. Place on a baking tray and cook for 5–6 minutes. Remove from the oven and cut into pieces.

Mix all the other salad ingredients in a large bowl with the dressing. Arrange the salad on serving plates and top with the hot crostini.

 Adrian recommends: ASK Italian's Bianco Salento.

A surprisingly rich salad with a herb dressing and touch of spice. It works wonderfully with our Bianco Salento: the Sauvignon complements the goat's cheese and the richness of the wine is more than a match for the bold salad flavours.

TONNO E FAGIOLI

TUNA AND BEAN SALAD

SERVES 4-6 / PREP: 10 MINUTES / COOK: NONE

Carla says: Another quintessentially Italian combo. This is the genius of Italian cooking: even when there's nothing in the fridge, you can rustle up a great and nutritious salad from the tins in the larder! If you are trying to help save the world's tuna, use mackerel or other tinned fish. This salad can be used as an antipasto too.

2 x 400g tins cannellini or borlotti beans

2 x 175g tins tuna fish, drained

4 tablespoons extra virgin olive oil

2 tablespoons fresh lemon juice

1 tablespoon finely chopped fresh parsley

1 tablespoon capers, drained

3 spring onions, thinly sliced

½ red onion, thinly sliced

salt and freshly ground black pepper

mixed salad leaves

Empty the beans into a large strainer and rinse well under cold water. Drain well. Place in a serving bowl.

Break the fish into fairly large flakes and arrange over the beans.

Make the dressing in a small bowl by mixing the olive oil with the lemon juice. Season with salt and pepper and stir in the parsley and capers. Mix well. Pour over the beans and tuna.

Sprinkle with the onions. Toss well before serving. Arrange on a bed of mixed leaves.

INSALATA DI SALMONE

SMOKED SALMON SALAD

SERVES 1 / PREP: 15 MINUTES / COOK: 2-3 MINUTES

We've recently launched this salad on our menu and our customers are loving it. It's a healthy main meal salad that's quick and easy to prepare. Hot-smoked salmon has lots of flavour and makes a great alternative to cold-smoked salmon. Peppadew peppers are small and slighty fiery: you'll find them at the deli counter or in jars. Double the quantities if you want to share your salad with a friend.

50g Cos lettuce, cut into 1cm slices

30g baby spinach leaves

3 baby plum tomatoes, halved

3 cucumber slices, cut into strips

2 yellow pepper rings, quartered

2 radishes, cut into wedges

3 Peppadew peppers, quartered

1 hot-smoked salmon fillet (85–100g), skinned and flaked into 8 pieces

60g Creamy Herb Dressing (see page 178)

1 x 1cm slice sourdough or Altamura bread

wedge of lemon

In a large bowl, combine all the salad vegetables and the salmon. Toss well with the dressing.

Toast the bread and cut into 4 pieces. Mix the toast pieces into the salad, and serve with a lemon wedge.

INSALATA DI POLLO E PANCETTA

CHICKEN SALAD WITH PANCETTA
SERVES 2 / PREP: 15 MINUTES / COOK: 5-10 MINUTES

Pancetta is Italy's answer to bacon: salt-cured pork belly that is sometimes also smoked. It has more depth of flavour than bacon, and marries well with the chicken in this substantial salad.

HONEY AND MUSTARD DRESSING:

100ml water

2 tablespoons white wine vinegar

2 tablespoons clear honey

½ teaspoon granulated sugar

2 tablespoons Dijon mustard

275ml ASK Italian extra virgin olive oil

2½ tablespoons wholegrain mustard

salt to taste

Makes approximately 500ml with 10 minutes preparation time. Place the water, vinegar, honey, sugar and Dijon mustard into a food processor and whizz to obtain a runny paste. Pour the oil in a slow stream into the processor while it is running. The dressing will start to emulsify and thicken. When all the oil has been added, stir in the wholegrain mustard and mix well. Taste for seasoning, adding salt as needed. This dressing will keep in a jar in the fridge for up to 2 weeks.

SALAD:

2 chicken breasts, skinned

2 tablespoons ASK Italian extra virgin olive oil

120g pancetta, cubed or cut into small sticks

100g Cos lettuce, sliced into 1cm strips

40g baby spinach leaves

½ an avocado, cubed

8 baby plum tomatoes, halved

6 red onion rings, halved

120ml (8 tablespoons) Honey and Mustard Dressing (see above)

To butterfly the chicken, place one chicken breast on a cutting board. With a sharp knife, cut the breast horizontally, leaving a 1cm strip along the long edge of the breast uncut. Open the breast out, so that it looks like two pages of a book joined at the seam. Repeat with the second breast.

Heat the oil in a non-stick frying pan large enough to hold both breasts open. Cook the chicken for 2 minutes on each side, turning it only once. Check that it is cooked through by making a little incision in the thickest part and, if necessary, cook for a minute or two more. Don't overcook or the chicken will dry out. Remove from the pan and allow the meat to rest for a minute before slicing into chunky strips.

In a smaller frying pan, slowly cook the pancetta until it releases some of its fat and becomes golden and crispy. You won't need to add oil to the pan. Transfer the pancetta to a piece of paper towel to drain.

In a mixing bowl toss the Cos, spinach, avocado, tomatoes and red onion with half of the dressing. Divide the salad between two serving plates. Top with the chicken and pancetta pieces. Drizzle with the remaining dressing before serving.

CHEF'S SALAD

We've given this classic all-in-one salad an Italian twist by using buffalo mozzarella, prosciutto, artichokes and olives in it instead of the usual cheese and ham. It makes a lovely party dish for lunch.

160g mixed salad leaves

4 ripe tomatoes, cut into wedges

¼ a cucumber, sliced thinly

½ a red or yellow pepper, sliced

4 tinned artichoke hearts, quartered

2 avocados, peeled and sliced

½ a red onion, thinly sliced into rings

20 pitted black olives

a small handful of fresh basil leaves, torn

200g buffalo mozzarella, torn into large pieces

6 tablespoons ASK Italian extra virgin olive oil

juice of ½ a lemon

4 x 1cm slices sourdough or Altamura bread

8 slices Speck or Parma ham

8 tablespoons freshly grated Parmesan or Grana Padano cheese

freshly ground sea salt and black pepper

In a large bowl, combine all the salad ingredients with the mozzarella. Dress with the olive oil and lemon juice, and season with salt and pepper.

Toast the bread and cut each slice into several large pieces. Top the salad with the sliced ham and grated cheese, and with chunks of toast.

CHICKEN CAESAR SALAD

SERVES 2 / PREP: 15 MINUTES / COOK: 4–6 MINUTES

This is a great salad for a summer's day. It's nutritious and quick to make. It is easy to butterfly the fresh chicken breasts, and this ensures that they cook more evenly.

2 chicken breasts, skinned

4 tablespoons ASK Italian extra virgin olive oil

2 x 1cm slices sourdough or Altamura bread

160g Cos lettuce, sliced into 1cm strips

8 tablespoons Caesar Dressing (see page 178)

20g Parmesan or Grana Padano cheese

To butterfly, place one chicken breast on a cutting board. With a sharp knife, cut the breast horizontally, leaving a 1cm strip along the long edge of the breast uncut. Open the breast out, so that it looks like two pages of a book joined at the seam. Repeat with the second breast.

Heat the oil in a non-stick frying pan large enough to hold both breasts open. Cook the chicken for 2 minutes on each side, turning it only once. Check that it is cooked through by making a little incision in the thickest part and, if necessary, cook for a minute or two more. Don't overcook or the chicken will dry out. Remove from the pan and allow the meat to rest for a minute before slicing into chunky strips.

While the chicken is cooking, toast the bread and cut each slice into three pieces.

Toss the lettuce with the dressing. Divide between two serving bowls, stacking the salad high on the plate. Top with the strips of chicken and the toast. Finish with shavings of cheese before serving.

VERDURE AL FORNO

ROASTED MIXED VEGETABLES

SERVES 4 / PREP: 15 MINUTES / COOK: 1 HOUR

Anna Stanton is the Head of Design for ASK Italian. Her Italian grandmother handed this recipe down to Anna's mother and to Anna. A panful of these colourful vegetables popped into the oven while you are roasting chicken or beef will make a great accompaniment for them. Anna says: 'My nonna's recipe is in the true southern Italian tradition known as "l'arte di arrangiarsi". ' This is the art of making the best of what you have to hand. In this case it results in a delicious, flexible recipe for whatever vegetables are available in the house — or vegetable garden. So, if you don't have carrots but do have potatoes, slice some into the pan with the other veggies.

1 aubergine

1 medium onion, cut through the base into 8 wedges

2 red or yellow peppers, sliced

2 carrots, sliced

3 tomatoes, quartered

2 parsnips, quartered

4 tablespoons extra virgin olive oil

1 tablespoon chopped fresh parsley

2 garlic cloves, peeled

1 teaspoon salt

Slice the aubergine into 2cm sticks. Sprinkle with salt and leave in a colander for 20 minutes to drain. Squeeze gently to remove excess water.

Preheat the oven to 200°C/400°F/gas mark 6.

Mix all the vegetables in a baking dish with the olive oil and parsley, making sure the vegetables are coated with oil. Lightly crush the garlic and add it to the vegetables. Bake for 1 hour, stirring and turning the vegetables every 15 minutes.

Anna Stanton

PISELLI CON PANCETTA

PEAS WITH PANCETTA

SERVES 4 / PREP: 10 MINUTES / COOK: 20 MINUTES

This is a lovely side dish, rich in flavour from the pancetta but very easy to prepare. Anna says: 'I love Italian cooking for the way it transforms simple, everyday ingredients into such tasty recipes.'

1 medium onion, finely chopped

2 tablespoons extra virgin olive oil

450g frozen peas

2 tablespoons finely chopped fresh parsley

200g pancetta, chopped

Sauté the onion in the oil until soft and translucent in a medium saucepan. Stir in the frozen peas and parsley. Cook for 5 minutes. Add the pancetta and cook for a further 15 minutes, stirring occasionally.

PEPERONATA

STEWED PEPPERS

SERVES 6 / PREP: 10 MINUTES / COOK: 35 MINUTES

Carla says: This southern Italian dish makes the best of the summer's ripest peppers. Use red, yellow and orange peppers, but not the unripe green ones. Peperonata is good as a side dish or antipasto and makes a delicious stuffing for frittatas and sandwiches.

4 or 5 (about 750g) ripe mixed large peppers
2 medium red onions, thinly sliced
4 tablespoons extra virgin olive oil
3 garlic cloves, halved
350g plum tomatoes, peeled and de-seeded
a few leaves of fresh basil, torn
salt and freshly ground black pepper

Wash the peppers. Cut them into quarters, removing the stems and seeds. Slice them into thin strips.

In a large heavy saucepan sauté the onions in the oil over a low heat until soft. Add the peppers, and cook for 5–8 minutes over a moderate heat, stirring frequently.

Stir in the garlic and tomatoes. Cover the pan, and cook for about 25 minutes, stirring occasionally. The peppers should be soft but should not lose their shape. Season to taste with salt and pepper and stir in the basil. Serve hot or cold.

FAGIOLINI VERDI CON POMODORO

GREEN BEANS WITH TOMATOES

SERVES 4 / PREP: 10 MINUTES / COOK: 35 MINUTES

Carla says: I love Italian vegetable dishes. These beans cook with the tomatoes so they lose none of their texture or flavours. Make this with fresh tomatoes in summer.

450g fresh green beans
3 tablespoons extra virgin olive oil
1 medium red onion, very finely sliced
325g fresh ripe or tinned plum tomatoes, peeled and finely chopped
250ml water
10 fresh basil leaves, torn into large pieces
salt and freshly ground black pepper

Snap or cut the stem end off the beans and discard. Wash the beans well in cold water and drain.

Heat the oil in a large frying pan with a lid. Add the onion and cook over a low heat until just soft, 5–6 minutes. Add the tomatoes, and cook over a moderate heat until they soften, 6–8 minutes.

Stir in the water and basil. Season the sauce with salt and pepper. Stir in the beans, turning them in the pan to coat with the sauce. Cover the pan and cook over a moderate heat until tender, about 15–20 minutes. Stir occasionally, adding a little more water if the sauce dries out too much. Serve hot or cold.

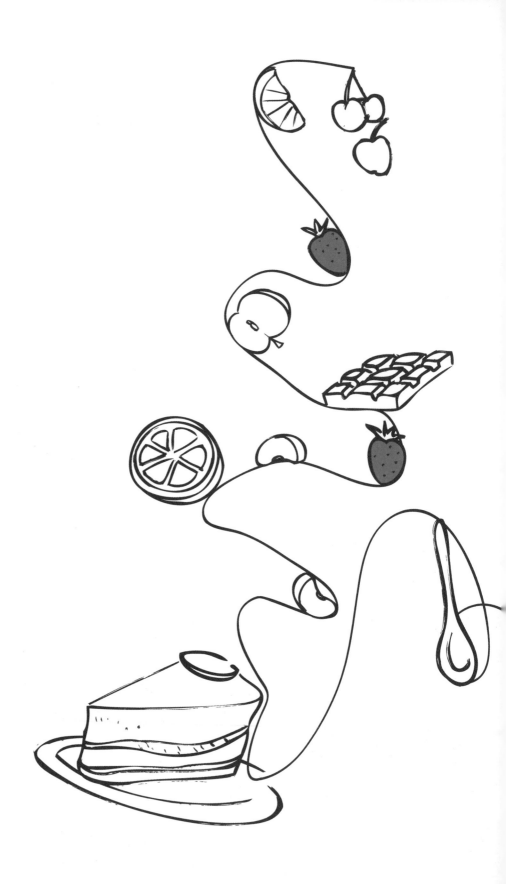

CHAPTER 7
DOLCI: DESSERTS

Finish your meal in true Italian style. We've brought together recipes for scrumptious ASK Italian cakes and tarts and feature them with ideas for jazzing up fruit salad, coffee and gelato.

TORTA MORBIDA DI CIOCCOLATO

SOFT CHOCOLATE CAKE WITH CREMA DI MASCARPONE
SERVES 8 / PREP: 25 MINUTES / COOK: 50-60 MINUTES

Theo says: This cake is unique. It looks like it might be heavy and dense, but it's actually light and amazingly chocolatey. If you don't have a bain-marie for your oven, improvise by using a deep baking dish – Pyrex works well – and a cake tin that won't leak. The cake tin needs to be standing in at least 5cm of water as it bakes so it doesn't burn.

CHOCOLATE CAKE:

400g 70% Valhrona chocolate

6 large eggs, at room temperature

150g caster sugar

300ml double cream

Preheat the oven to 150°C/300°F/gas mark 2.

Place a bain-marie (or glass or ceramic baking dish large enough to stand a cake tin in) in the oven. Butter and line a waterproof 20cm round cake tin with parchment paper. Melt the chocolate in a bowl placed over a saucepan of simmering water. Don't let the water touch the bowl. Remove from the heat when the chocolate has melted.

Meanwhile, separate the eggs. Whisk the yolks with 100g of the sugar until pale yellow in a medium bowl. Stir in the melted chocolate. In another bowl, whip 150ml of cream with a whisk until the cream forms soft peaks.

In a large clean mixing bowl, whisk the egg whites until they form soft peaks, adding the remaining 50g of sugar gradually. The egg whites should be glossy and light, like a meringue mixture.

Stir the remaining 150ml of unwhipped cream into the chocolate mixture. Fold in the whipped cream. Carefully fold in the egg whites and pour into the prepared tin.

Place the tin in the bain-marie. The water level should be at least 5–10cm high. Bake for approximately 50–60 minutes. The cake should be firm on top with a slight wobble. Allow to cool and serve, sliced, at room temperature, with the Crema di Mascarpone.

CREMA DI MASCARPONE:

150g double cream

200g mascarpone

scraped-out seeds of ½ a vanilla pod

50g icing sugar, or to taste

25ml Marsala wine, or to taste

Mix all the ingredients together in a bowl. Add sugar and Marsala to taste. Serve with the cake.

TORTA AI FRUTTI DI BOSCO

MIXED BERRY TART

SERVES 8-10 / PREP: 1 HOUR 30 MINUTES INCLUDING PASTRY / COOK: 45 MINUTES

Frutti di bosco are wood berries, so you can top this custard tart with all your favourite soft fruit. In winter we top it with stewed apricots and soaked raisins for a holiday treat. These tarts have been featured on our Specials menu and are always popular. If you're short of time, use a shop-bought pastry case and fill with the custard and fruits.

SHORTCRUST PASTRY CASE:

225g plain flour

100g icing sugar

125g butter, chilled

2 large egg yolks

2 tablespoons water

salt

CUSTARD:

300ml milk

1 vanilla pod, slit lengthways and seeds scraped out

2 large egg yolks

40g granulated sugar

35g cornflour

150g mascarpone

TOPPING:

100g strawberries, quartered

100g raspberries

100g blueberries

icing sugar for dusting

First make the shortcrust pastry. If you're making the pastry by hand, place the flour, sugar and a pinch of salt in a mixing bowl. Using a pastry blender or two knives, cut the butter into the dry ingredients as quickly as possible until the mixture resembles coarse meal. Using a fork, stir in the egg yolks and water. Gather the dough into a ball. Flatten the ball into a disc and cover with greaseproof paper. Refrigerate for at least 1 hour.

Alternatively, place the dry ingredients in the food processor with the chilled butter cut into small cubes. Pulse the processor until the mixture resembles coarse crumbs. Stir the water into the egg yolks and add to the butter mixture, pulsing the processor until the mixture begins to come together. Remove the dough from the processor, forming it quickly into a ball. Flatten the ball into a disc and cover with greaseproof paper. Refrigerate for at least 1 hour.

Lightly grease a shallow 28–30cm tart or pie tin, preferably with a removable bottom. Remove the chilled dough from the fridge and place it on a lightly floured surface. Roll out the dough to a thickness of 5mm in a circle a bit larger than the tin. Roll the pastry around the rolling pin and transfer it to the prepared tin. Trim the edges evenly with a small knife. Prick the pastry all over with a fork. Refrigerate for at least 30 minutes.

Preheat the oven to 180°C/350°F/gas mark 4.

Bake for 10–12 minutes or until lightly brown. Remove from the oven and cool on a wire rack.

To make the custard, gently heat the milk in a heavy-bottomed saucepan with the vanilla pod and seeds until it barely comes to the boil. Remove from the heat. Remove the pod.

Mix the egg yolks, sugar and cornflour together in a bowl until pale and fluffy. Slowly whisk in half the milk in a steady stream. Pour the egg mixture into the saucepan with the rest of the milk. Cook over a low heat for 3–4 minutes until the mixture thickens, stirring constantly.

Spoon the custard into a bowl, cover with clingfilm to prevent a skin forming, and refrigerate. When the custard is cool, fold in the mascarpone.

Assemble the tart by spreading the custard evenly over the base of the pastry shell. Top with the berries and a dusting of icing sugar before serving. If you prefer, you can top the tart with apricots and raisins in amaretto syrup (see page 183).

GELATO CON FRUTTA COTTA

GELATO WITH STEWED FRUITS

SERVES 4 / PREP: 10 MINUTES / COOK: NONE

We love this simple dessert that's unusual and elegant enough to show off at a dinner party. Apricots and raisins are stewed in almond liqueur and served over vanilla gelato. In Italy, restaurants have to compete with fabulous gelaterie, so they create imaginative gelato-based desserts to entice their customers to stay at their tables a little longer (and we do the same).

½ the recipe for Apricots and Raisins in Amaretto Syrup (see page 183)

4 scoops vanilla gelato

100g fresh raspberries

4g flaked almonds

icing sugar, for dusting

Prepare the apricot and raisin mixture in advance.

Choose your prettiest sundae glasses or decorative bowls for this dessert. Just before you're ready to serve, scoop some vanilla gelato into each glass. Divide the apricot and raisin mixture between the glasses. Top with a few raspberries and a scattering of flaked almonds. Dust with icing sugar and serve immediately.

TORTA DI MELA E FRANGIPANE

APPLE RUSTICA TARTS

SERVES 4 / PREP: 1 HOUR INCLUDING PASTRY / COOK: 40 MINUTES

These little apple tarts have always been favourites on our menu. They're filled with frangipane, a sweet almond cream we like to make from Italian almonds. They're good cold or warm, especially when served with vanilla gelato. If you don't have time to make your own pastry, use uncooked ready-made pastry.

FRANGIPANE:

40g butter

50g caster sugar

1 large egg

½ teaspoon pure vanilla essence

50g ground almonds

12g plain flour

SHORTCRUST PASTRY:

225g plain flour

100g icing sugar

125g butter, chilled

2 large egg yolks

2 tablespoons water

salt

APPLE MIX:

40g butter, at room temperature

40g caster sugar

2 apples, peeled, cored and cut into thin slices

To make the frangipane, cream the butter and sugar together in a large bowl until the mixture is pale yellow and fluffy. Beat in the egg. Add the vanilla essence. Fold in the ground almonds and flour. Mix well and chill until needed.

Make the shortcrust pastry following the instructions on page 160. Divide it into 4 balls, flatten them into discs and cover with greaseproof paper or clingfilm. Refrigerate for 1 hour.

Lightly grease 4 shallow 10–15cm tart or pie pans, preferably with removable bottoms. Remove the chilled dough from the fridge and place on a lightly floured surface. Roll out the dough to a thickness of 5mm in a circle a bit larger than the tin. Transfer to the prepared tin. Trim the edges evenly with a small knife. Prick the pastry all over with a fork. Repeat with the other discs. Refrigerate while you prepare the apples.

Preheat the oven to 190°C/375°F/gas mark 5.

Cream the butter and sugar together into a paste. Add the apple slices, stirring them to coat with the sugar mixture. Don't worry if they break.

Split the apple mixture between the pastry cases. Divide the frangipane between the tarts, spreading it evenly over the apples with a spatula. Bake for 35–40 minutes or until the crust is golden brown. Remove from the oven and allow to cool on a wire rack before serving.

TORTA ITALIANA

PRUNE, PISTACHIO AND ALMOND CAKE

SERVES UP TO 10 / PREP: 40 MINUTES / COOK: 35-40 MINUTES

This cake is easy to make for a family gathering, and stars prunes as well as Sicilian pistachios and almonds. Frangipane is a sweet almond cream that features in many fruit tarts. You could substitute soft dried apricots for the prunes if you prefer. We like to serve this cake warm with a scoop of vanilla gelato.

FRANGIPANE:

180g butter

180g caster sugar

3 large eggs

20g freshly squeezed lemon juice

150g ground almonds

60g plain flour

BISCUIT:

200g digestive biscuits, crushed

90g muscovado or molasses sugar

90g butter

TOPPING:

250g soft semi-dried prunes, pitted

30g sliced almonds

20g chopped pistachios

To make the frangipane, cream the butter and sugar together in a large bowl until the mixture is pale yellow and fluffy. Beat in the eggs, one at a time. Add the lemon juice. Fold in the ground almonds and flour. Mix well and chill until needed.

Preheat the oven to 190°C/375°F/gas mark 5.

To make the biscuit base, butter a 23–25cm x 6cm shallow cake or tart tin, preferably with a removable bottom. Stir the biscuit crumbs and brown sugar together in a mixing bowl. Rub in the butter until you have the consistency of coarse breadcrumbs. Turn the crumb mixture into the baking tin, patting it down evenly.

Arrange the soft prunes on the biscuit base and spoon the frangipane on top, smoothing it with a spatula to make the cake level. Sprinkle with the flaked almonds and pistachios. Bake for 35–40 minutes. Allow the cake to cool before serving.

 Adrian recommends: ASK Italian's Recioto di Soave.

This is a rich, sweet and complex dish that is perfectly complemented by our dessert wine which is similarly sweet and shows wonderful complex nutty flavours as a result of prolonged barrel aging.

PESCHE ALLA PIEMONTESE

BAKED PEACHES WITH AMARETTI STUFFING

SERVES 4 / PREP: 15 MINUTES / COOK: 40 MINUTES

Carla says: This is one of my all-time favourite fruit desserts, from Piedmont in north-western Italy. It's so easy to make, yet is special enough for a dinner party. I love these peaches served hot with whipped cream or yogurt, but they are good cold too, with ice cream. Make them when peaches are in season.

4 ripe fresh peaches

juice of ½ a lemon

65g amaretti biscuits, crushed

2 tablespoons Marsala, brandy or peach brandy

25g butter, at room temperature

½ teaspoon vanilla extract

2 tablespoons sugar

1 egg yolk

Preheat the oven to 180°C/350°F/gas mark 4.

Wash the peaches. Cut them in half and remove the stones. Enlarge the hollow left by the stones by scooping out some of the peach with a small spoon. Sprinkle the peach halves with the lemon juice.

Mash the scooped-out peach pieces with a fork. Soften the amaretti crumbs in the liqueur for a few minutes. Beat 25g of the butter until soft. Stir in the amaretti mixture. Combine with the mashed peach. Stir in the remaining ingredients.

Arrange the peach halves on a baking tray in one layer. Divide the amaretti mixture into 8, and fill the hollows, mounding the stuffing up in the centre. Dot the tops with the remaining butter. Bake for 35–40 minutes. Serve hot or cold.

MACEDONIA

FRUIT SALAD

SERVES 4-6 / PREP: 20 MINUTES / COOK: NONE

Carla says: Italian fruit salad is never dry because the Italians like to freshen up their cut fruits with freshly squeezed orange and lemon juice. Use all your favourite seasonal fruits and berries in this healthy dessert and serve it with gelato or yogurt.

juice of 2 sweet oranges

juice of 1 lemon

2 apples

1 ripe pear

2 peaches or nectarines

1 banana

4 or 5 apricots or plums

110g black or green grapes

110g blueberries or other berries

sugar (optional)

Kirsch or maraschino or other liqueur (optional)

Pour the fresh orange and lemon juices into a large serving bowl.

Prepare the fruits by washing or peeling them as necessary and cutting them into bite-size pieces. Halve the grapes and remove any seeds. Leave small berries whole. As soon as each fruit has been prepared, put it into the bowl with the juices.

Taste the salad, adding sugar if you like it sweeter. For grown-up dinner parties, you can also add a splash of liqueur. Cover the bowl and refrigerate until serving. Gently stir the fruit again before serving.

TORTA AL LIMONE

LEMON TART WITH MERINGUE

SERVES UP TO 10 / PREP: 40 MINUTES PLUS 1 HOUR FOR PASTRY / COOK: 15 MINUTES

The Italians grow some of the world's best citrus fruit in Sicily, and they love to use lemons in their desserts. In the UK, lemon tart wouldn't be complete without a soft meringue topping. So here's our Anglo-Italian favourite.

SHORTCRUST PASTRY CASE:

225g plain flour

100g icing sugar

125g butter

2 large egg yolks

2 tablespoons water

salt

LEMON CUSTARD:

300g caster sugar

300ml fresh lemon juice

6 large egg yolks

45g cornflour

grated zest of 3 lemons

MERINGUE:

6 large egg whites

75g caster sugar

75g icing sugar

salt

To make baked shortcrust pastry case, follow the instructions on page 160.

Next make the lemon custard. In a heavy-bottomed saucepan, mix the sugar into the lemon juice and bring it gently to the boil over a low heat. In a mixing bowl, whisk the egg yolks and cornflour together. Pour in the hot lemon mixture in a slow stream. Pour the mixture back into the saucepan and cook gently over a low heat for 3–4 minutes until it thickens, whisking constantly. Stir in the lemon zest.

Pour the custard into a bowl, cover with clingfilm to prevent a skin from forming, and chill.

To make the meringue, use an electric beater to whisk the egg whites with a pinch of salt and a spoonful of the caster sugar in a large clean glass or ceramic bowl until the mixture is fluffy and forms stiff peaks when the blades are lifted. Beat in the rest of the caster sugar, one dessertspoonful at a time, beating for a few seconds after each addition. The egg whites will be glossy and thick.

Sift one-third of the icing sugar over the meringue and gently fold it in using a clean spatula or large metal spoon. Continue with the rest of the icing sugar, taking care not to over-mix.

Turn on the grill.

Assemble the tart by spreading the lemon custard evenly over the base of the pastry case. Spoon the meringue on top, smoothing the edges to seal it and making soft peaks with the back of a spoon. Put the meringue under the grill for 2–3 minutes or until the meringue starts to become golden. Allow to cool and refrigerate until serving. Serve with a tablespoon of crème fraîche on each plate if you wish.

Adrian recommends: ASK Italian's Moscato d'Asti.

This lightly sparkling Italian speciality really brings this dessert to life. It's brimming with citrus fruit and is light, clean and refreshing: it's the perfect way to end a meal.

AFFOGATO AL CAFFÈ

HOT COFFEE AND ICE CREAM
SERVES 1 / PREP: 5 MINUTES / COOK: NONE

This is a neat little trick that you can find in every Italian bar or coffee shop: it turns an espresso coffee into a delicious dessert in one second. Affogato means 'drowned', and what could be nicer for a scoop of cold vanilla gelato than to be drowned in a tiny cupful of aromatic hot espresso? It's a great way to show off your Italian coffee pot, so try it for dessert or for a quick afternoon treat.

1 scoop vanilla gelato

2 Cantuccini biscuits

1 espresso

Make sure you have everything ready before you make the espresso as it needs to be piping hot. Put a scoop of vanilla gelato in a serving bowl. Arrange the biscuits on a plate. Make the coffee and pour it over the gelato. Enjoy it right away!

TIRAMISÙ

COFFEE AND MASCARPONE DESSERT
SERVES 4-6 / PREP: 30 MINUTES / COOK: 2 HOURS

This has to be Italy's favourite dessert, and it is one of the best sellers in our restaurants. The coffee, alcohol and deliciously creamy mascarpone cheese give the dish its power as a 'pick me up'. The original Savoiardi biscuits it's made with are from Piedmont, and are thicker than most lady fingers, but either kind will do. If you want to make it child-friendly, use decaffeinated coffee and leave out the alcohol.

400g mascarpone cheese

5 large eggs, separated

120g caster sugar

200g Savoiardi or lady finger biscuits

200ml espresso coffee, at room temperature

30ml Marsala wine, brandy or rum

cocoa powder

salt

In a small bowl, beat the mascarpone cheese until it is soft. In a larger mixing bowl, beat the egg yolks with about two-thirds of the sugar until it is pale and creamy. Gradually beat in the softened mascarpone.

In another bowl beat the egg whites with the rest of the sugar and a pinch of salt until they form fairly stiff peaks. Gently fold the egg whites into the mascarpone mixture.

Mix the coffee and liqueur together. Line a serving bowl evenly with the biscuits in one layer. Drizzle with half the coffee mixture. Spoon half of the mascarpone mixture over the biscuits and smooth it into an even layer with a spatula. Repeat with another layer of biscuits, coffee and mascarpone.

Sprinkle the top with cocoa powder. Refrigerate the tiramisù for at least 2 hours before serving.

SPUMINI ALLE MANDORLE

ALMOND MERINGUES

SERVES 4-6 / PREP: 15 MINUTES / COOK: 30 MINUTES

Vito Ivone is our Operations Manager for ASK Italian in northern Scotland. He grew up in Puglia, in Italy's 'heel', came to Scotland as a young man, fell in love and has lived there ever since. He loves cooking for his extended family: 28 people when they are all gathered around the table! Vito says: 'This recipe reminds me of my Italian childhood. These almond meringues, whose name means "little foams", were made by my aunt Margherita who moved from Castellana Grotte in the south of Italy to Gorizia, in the north-east. She always baked them for us on birthdays and holidays. You can store them in an air-tight tin for over a week — if you can resist eating them first. Serve them with whipped cream, gelato or just by themselves.'

3 large egg whites, at room temperature

250g sugar

250g toasted blanched almonds, roughly chopped

Preheat the oven to 180°C/350°F/gas mark 4. Line a flat baking tray with parchment paper.

Using an electric whisk, beat the egg whites with 1 tablespoon of the sugar until they form stiff peaks. Using a flat spatula, fold in the rest of the sugar. Carefully fold in the almonds.

Using a teaspoon, drop spoonfuls of the mixture onto the baking tray, leaving enough room on the tray for them to expand. If you prefer bigger spumini, use a larger spoon. Bake for 30 minutes. The spumini will remain moist and chewy inside.

Vito Ivone (left) and friend

BIANCOMANGIARE AI PISTACCHI

BLANCMANGE WITH PISTACHIOS

SERVES 4-6 / PREP: 20 MINUTES / COOK: 15 MINUTES, WITH 1 HOUR CHILLING TIME

Marco Gambino is an actor who was born and raised in Sicily. He works with ASK Italian, telling stories about Italy and bringing the country and its culture to life for our teams. Marco says: 'Blancmange has rather fallen out of fashion in Great Britain, but in Sicily it is considered a delicacy. It was probably brought to the island during the Arab conquest in the Middle Ages. This recipe, with its hint of cinnamon and creamy texture, reminds me of my childhood in Palermo, when my mother would greet me after school with this delicious treat. "It will melt in your mouth," she would say. And it did.'

60g cornflour

1 litre fresh milk

zest of 1 lemon

1 vanilla pod, split in half lengthways

150g sugar

¼ teaspoon cinnamon

50g ground pistachios

In a medium saucepan, whisk the cornflour into the milk over a low heat. Stir in the lemon zest, vanilla pod and sugar. Turn up the heat to medium and bring the mixture to the boil, whisking constantly until the cream thickens.

Remove from the heat and allow the mixture to cool. Remove the vanilla pod (if you rinse it in cold water and dry it, you can store the pod and use it again). Divide the blancmange between 6 serving glasses. Sprinkle with a pinch of cinnamon and the pistachios. Refrigerate for at least 1 hour before serving.

Marco Gambino

GRANITA DI LIMONE

LEMON GRANITA
SERVES 6 / PREP: 10 MINUTES / FREEZING TIME: 2 HOURS

Carla says: Nothing is more refreshing on a hot summer's day than fresh lemon granita. It's like slushy frozen lemonade, and kids love drinking it with straws while the ice is melting. Use a food processor or power blender to chop the ice to the grainy frozen consistency. When you're grating the lemon rind, make sure you don't include the bitter white pith that is just below the yellow part.

125g sugar

500ml water

grated zest of 1 lemon, scrubbed before grating

juice of 2 large lemons

In a small saucepan, heat the sugar and water together over a low heat until the sugar dissolves. Bring to the boil briefly and then remove from the heat. Set the syrup aside to cool.

Stir the lemon zest and juice into the sugar syrup. Pour the mixture into a freezer tray, and freeze until solid.

Stand the bottom of the frozen tray in very hot water for a few seconds and turn the frozen mixture out onto a cutting board. Chop it into large chunks. Place them in the bowl of a food processor fitted with metal blades and process until the granita forms small crystals. Spoon into serving glasses and serve with a long spoon and a straw.

If you don't want to serve the granita immediately, pour the processed mixture back into an ice tray and freeze until you're ready to serve it. Allow it to thaw for a few minutes before serving, or process again.

GRANITA DI CAFFÈ

COFFEE GRANITA
SERVES 6 / PREP: 10 MINUTES / FREEZING TIME: 2 HOURS

Carla says: This coffee granita brings a new dimension to iced coffee. A granita is a cross between a frozen drink and a flavoured ice. The consistency should be slushy, and in Italy they are often made in machines which constantly churn the ice to stop it from freezing solid.

150g sugar

500ml water

250ml very strong espresso coffee, cooled

whipped cream (optional)

In a small saucepan, heat the sugar and water together over low heat until the sugar dissolves. Bring to the boil briefly and then remove from the heat. Set the syrup aside to cool.

Stir the coffee into the sugar syrup. Pour the mixture into a freezer tray, and freeze until solid.

Follow the same method as for the lemon granita, above.

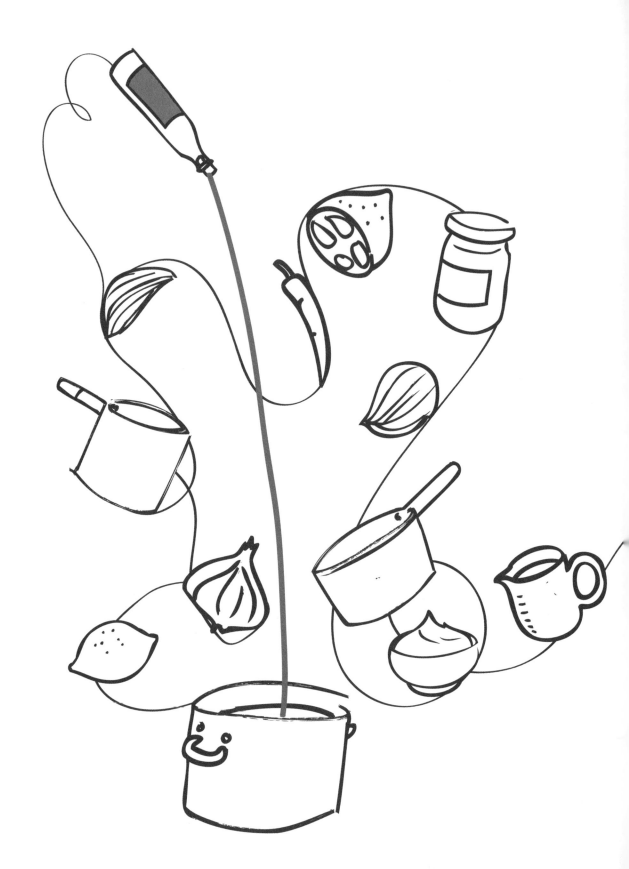

CHAPTER 8
SAUCES AND BASICS

In this chapter we'll be sharing useful recipes to make our ASK Italian staples, like creamy herb dressing, garlic butter and béchamel sauce.

CAESAR DRESSING

MAKES APPROX. 500ML / PREP: 30 MINUTES / COOK: NONE

1 garlic clove, finely chopped

1 anchovy fillet, finely chopped

2 tablespoons water

1 teaspoon cream cheese or cream

2 tablespoons ASK Italian extra virgin olive oil

1½ tablespoons white wine vinegar

1 tablespoon Worcestershire sauce

1 teaspoon lemon juice

½ teaspoon sugar

1 teaspoon wholegrain mustard

1 tablespoon grated Parmesan cheese

1 teaspoon Dijon mustard

325g mayonnaise

freshly ground sea salt and black pepper

Put the garlic, anchovy, water and cream cheese into a food processor and whizz to make a paste. Add all the other ingredients except the mayonnaise and process again. Turn the mixture into a bowl and whisk in the mayonnaise. Taste for seasoning, adding salt and pepper as needed.

CREAMY HERB DRESSING

MAKES APPROX. 400ML / PREP: 30 MINUTES / COOK: NONE

100ml water

60ml (4 tablespoons) fresh lemon juice

1 tablespoon Lilliput or other small capers

2 garlic cloves, finely chopped

1 teaspoon granulated sugar

a pinch of cayenne pepper

40g fresh flat-leaf parsley, finely chopped

115ml ASK Italian extra virgin olive oil

100g mayonnaise

1 tablespoon wholegrain mustard

1 tablespoon Dijon mustard

salt and freshly ground black pepper

Place the water, lemon juice, capers, garlic, sugar, ½ a teaspoon of salt, the cayenne pepper and half the parsley into a food processor. Process until smooth. Pour the oil in a slow stream into the processor while it is running. The dressing will start to emulsify and thicken. When all the oil has been added, switch off the processor.

Turn the sauce into a bowl and stir in the mayonnaise, mustards and the rest of the parsley. Taste for seasoning, adding a few grindings of black pepper if needed.

GARLIC BUTTER

MAKES APPROX. 100G / PREP: 20 MINUTES / COOK: NONE

We love garlic butter and always make it from top quality fresh ingredients. It's really easy to whip up a batch and keep it handy in the fridge.

12g garlic (about 3 cloves), finely chopped

2 pinches of ground sea salt

1 lemon wedge

100g unsalted butter, at room temperature

a few leaves of fresh flat-leaf parsley, finely chopped

Crush the garlic and salt to a paste in a mortar and pestle. Add a good squeeze of lemon juice and mix well.

Stir the butter in a small bowl with a wooden spoon until creamy. Add the garlic mixture and cream together. Stir in the parsley. That's it! Well covered, it will keep in the fridge for up to a week.

PESTO ALLA GENOVESE

GREEN BASIL PESTO

MAKES APPROX. 500G / PREP: 10 MINUTES / COOK: NONE

This is great not only on pasta, but also stirred into soups or used to brighten up sandwiches or even pizzas.

50g toasted pine nuts

100g (a large bunch) fresh basil leaves, stalks removed

100g Parmesan cheese, freshly grated

1 garlic clove, crushed with a little sea salt

60ml (4 tablespoons) water

150ml ASK Italian extra virgin olive oil

freshly ground sea salt and black pepper

Place the pine nuts, basil, Parmesan, garlic and water in the bowl of a blender or food processor and process for 45 seconds. Pour in the olive oil and whizz again for 20 seconds. Scrape the pesto into a bowl and season with salt and pepper to taste. Cover with cling film and store in the refrigerator until needed. It will keep in the fridge for a few days. Pesto also freezes well, and will last for a month. Make a pouch with kitchen foil, spoon the pesto into it and close before freezing.

BALSAMIC ONIONS

MAKES APPROX. 200G / PREP: 5 MINUTES / COOK: 5 MINUTES

1 medium onion, finely sliced

1 tablespoon ASK Italian extra virgin olive oil

1 tablespoon balsamic vinegar

salt

Heat the onions in a small frying pan over a low heat with the oil. Cook slowly until the onions are translucent, stirring to make sure they don't brown. Turn them into a bowl and stir in the vinegar and a pinch of salt.

SALSA DI FUNGHI

MUSHROOM SAUCE

SERVES 6-8 (MAKES APPROX. 750G) / PREP: 15 MINUTES / COOK: 30 MINUTES

This hearty mushroom sauce is used in several of our recipes and can also be used on its own as a pasta sauce. Just add a little cream to it for a more lustrous result.

10g dried porcini mushrooms

3 tablespoons ASK Italian extra virgin olive oil

30g white onion, chopped

20g celery, diced

2 garlic cloves, finely chopped

a pinch of ground fennel seeds

100g button mushrooms, finely chopped

550ml water

100ml chicken stock

1 teaspoon granulated sugar

1 tablespoon cornflour

60ml (4 tablespoons) milk

3 tablespoons finely chopped fresh flat-leaf parsley

1 tablespoon finely chopped fresh tarragon

freshly ground black pepper

Soak the porcini mushrooms in 100ml of warm water for 30 minutes. Strain the porcini, keeping their soaking water in a small bowl. Finely chop the porcini.

Heat the oil in a saucepan. Add the onion and celery and cook over a low heat for about 6 minutes, or until the onions are translucent. Add the garlic and the ground fennel. Stir in half of the chopped mushrooms and all of the porcini. Add half the water (275 ml) and simmer gently for 5 minutes, covered.

Meanwhile, in a small bowl, stir the reserved porcini water, chicken stock, sugar and cornflour into the remaining 275ml of water.

Remove the saucepan from the heat and, using a hand blender or food processor, blend until smooth. Return the saucepan to the heat and pour in the cornflour mixture, stirring with a whisk as you bring the sauce back up to simmering. The sauce should thicken slightly.

Add the milk, herbs and remaining mushrooms. Simmer for a further 10 minutes. Use the sauce hot or allow it to cool before storing it in the fridge for up to 3 days.

VEGETABLE STOCK

MAKES 1.5 LITRES / PREP: 5 MINUTES / COOK: 40 MINUTES

This is Theo Randall's easy vegetable stock. Use it as a base for soups or risotto.

2 carrots, peeled

2 celery sticks

1 leek, split and washed thoroughly

a sprig of thyme

a bunch of fresh flat-leaf parsley

1 bay leaf

2 litres cold water

1 teaspoon sea salt

3 white peppercorns

Place all the ingredients including the water in a large saucepan. Bring the pan to the boil and skim off any foam. Reduce the heat and simmer for 30–40 minutes, depending on how strong you want the stock to be.

When the stock is ready, remove the vegetables and pass the stock though a fine sieve. Make sure the stock is cold before you place it in the fridge as it will go sour very quickly. The stock can be kept for 2-3 days in the fridge.

BOLOGNESE SAUCE

MEAT SAUCE

PREP: 20 MINUTES / COOK: 1 HOUR 30 MINUTES

This makes enough for 4 generous portions of sauce. If you want more, just double the quantities and follow the same instructions, allowing a bit more time for the sauce's final slow simmering.

4 tablespoons ASK Italian extra virgin olive oil

130g (1 large) white onion, finely chopped

450g lean minced beef

4 garlic cloves, finely chopped

100ml red wine

150ml beef stock

1 x 400g tin chopped tomatoes

500g tomato passata

5 fresh basil leaves, finely chopped

2 tablespoons finely chopped fresh flat-leaf parsley

1 teaspoon dried oregano

2 tablespoons Worcestershire sauce

juice of ½ a lemon

½ teaspoon salt

freshly ground black pepper

Heat the oil in a saucepan over a low heat, add the onion and cook slowly until it has softened and become translucent.

Add the beef mince and brown gently, breaking the meat up with a fork and stirring constantly. When the meat has lost its raw look, add the garlic. Add the wine, turn up the heat and cook for about 5 minutes, until the wine has evaporated.

Stir in the stock, tomatoes and passata. Season with the herbs, Worcestershire sauce, lemon juice and salt. Bring to the boil and cook for 5 minutes, stirring often. Check the seasoning, adding pepper to taste.

Lower the heat and cook the sauce very gently for 1 hour 20 minutes with the lid off. Stir often to prevent the sauce from sticking. It should be at a slow simmer. When the sauce is done, either serve it on hot pasta or allow to cool before covering and storing in the fridge. It will keep well for several days. Heat gently to simmering point before serving.

BÉCHAMEL SAUCE

MAKES ENOUGH TO MAKE 1 TRAY OF LASAGNE / PREP: 35 MINUTES / COOK: 5–6 MINUTES

The Italians and the French both lay claim to having invented this classic white sauce. The Italians call it besciamella, like béchamel with an Italian accent. Wherever it comes from, we're happy to have it for our home-made lasagne!

125g butter

125g plain flour

1.1 litre semi-skimmed milk

½ teaspoon freshly ground black pepper

½ teaspoon freshly ground sea salt

Melt the butter in a large saucepan and whisk in the flour. Cook for 2 minutes over a low heat, stirring constantly. Add the milk in a slow, steady stream, stirring to prevent lumps. The sauce will thicken as it cooks. When the sauce has come to the boil, season with salt and pepper and cook for 1 minute more.

Remove the pan from the heat and either stand it in cold water to cool, or transfer the sauce to a bowl. Allow it to cool down for 20 minutes before covering the bowl with cling film to help prevent a skin forming. If you are not using the béchamel right away, refrigerate it until needed.

CHILLI OIL

MAKES APPROX. 500ML / PREP: 5 MINUTES / COOK: NONE

We love to serve this with all our pizzas, because some do like it hot. Chillies vary a lot, so always taste a few drops before putting it on your pizza as this oil can be pretty fiery!

5–10 whole dried red chillies

25g black peppercorns

25g chilli flakes

500ml ASK Italian extra virgin olive oil

Mix all the ingredients in the olive oil in a glass jar, cover, and allow to infuse for at least 2 weeks in the larder. This will keep for several months, but remember it will keep getting hotter.

SALSA VERDE

PARSLEY AND CAPER SAUCE

MAKES APPROX. 130G (10 TABLESPOONS) / PREP: 10 MINUTES / COOK: NONE

The best way to make salsa verde is to chop all the ingredients very finely by hand. If you don't have time, put them into a blender or food processor and whizz until smooth. This sauce goes very well with roast meat.

30g fresh flat-leaf parsley

1 garlic clove

1 tablespoon Lilliput or other small capers, drained

1 tablespoon lemon juice

120ml ASK Italian extra virgin olive oil

freshly ground sea salt and black pepper

Chop the parsley, garlic and capers very finely by hand.

Stir in the lemon juice and olive oil. Taste for seasoning. You can store the sauce in the fridge for a few days in an airtight jar.

PEELED GRILLED PEPPERS

PREP: 15 MINUTES / COOK: 20 MINUTES

Several of our recipes call for peeled red or yellow peppers. You can buy them now quite easily in jars, but it's also very simple to prepare your own and the smoky flavours from the grill make them taste fantastic.

Turn on your oven grill.

Line a baking sheet with foil. Lay the peppers on it in one layer and place under the hot grill. As the skins blacken and blister, turn the peppers over to grill the other sides. The peppers should be black all over.

Remove from the heat and place in a paper or plastic bag for a few minutes. This helps to steam loose any remaining attached skin. Peel the peppers: in a shallow bowl, pull them open and discard the seeds and stalks. Save the liquid for use in a sauce or soup. Slice the peppers lengthways into thin narrow strips.

SAUTÉED MUSHROOMS

MAKES 440G, ENOUGH FOR 4 PIZZAS / PREP: 10 MINUTES / COOK: 8-10 MINUTES

This versatile mushroom mix is featured in several of our recipes, from pizza to pasta.

4 tablespoons ASK Italian extra virgin olive oil

100g (1 large) portobello mushroom, sliced

125g (5) button mushrooms, sliced

125g (5) chestnut mushrooms, sliced

125g (10) oyster mushrooms, sliced

1 garlic clove, finely chopped

1 teaspoon chopped fresh thyme

freshly ground sea salt and black pepper

Heat the oil in a medium frying pan. Add the mushrooms and sauté over a medium heat for 5–6 minutes until they start to soften.

Stir in the garlic and thyme. Season to taste with salt and pepper. Lower the heat and cook for a couple of minutes more, stirring to prevent the mushrooms from sticking.

PANGRATTATO

TOASTED HERB-SCENTED BREADCRUMBS
FOR 4 HANDFULS (30G) / PREP: 5 MINUTES / COOK: 5-6 MINUTES

30g (2 thin slices) sourdough or Altamura bread

1 tablespoon ASK Italian extra virgin olive oil

a pinch of dried wild oregano

salt and freshly ground black pepper

Preheat the oven to 220°C/425°F/gas mark 7.

Tear the bread, including the crust, into tiny pieces. Mix with the olive oil and oregano, and season to taste.

Spread the torn bread onto an oiled baking tray and toast in a hot oven for 5–6 minutes. Allow to cool before using as a garnish.

APRICOTS AND RAISINS IN AMARETTO SYRUP

SERVES 8 / PREP: 10 MINUTES / COOK: 10 MINUTES

Use this delicious mixture for topping gelati or as an alternative topping for the Torta ai Frutti di Bosco (see page 160). Scatter with flaked almonds and dust with icing sugar before serving.

140ml water

45g sugar, white or light brown

90g dried apricots, diced

25g raisins

3 tablespoons amaretto liqueur

Pour the water into a small heavy saucepan and add the sugar, stirring over a low heat until the sugar has dissolved.

Stir in the apricots, raisins and amaretto liqueur. Simmer for 5-7 minutes until the ingredients have had time to amalgamate. Allow to cool to room temperature before serving. You can keep this mixture in the fridge for a week.

ACKNOWLEDGEMENTS

Creating a book is always a collaborative effort, especially when it involves so many recipes and photographs. We'd like to thank the many people who have played a part in producing it.

ASK Italian's expert friends have had key roles in this book. Chef Theo Randall is the creative inspiration behind ASK Italian's menu and he has generously shared his enthusiasm for cooking Italian food and given us a number of his favourite recipes for the book. Author and photographer Carla Capalbo has worn many hats on this project: as well as editing the recipes and offering creative guidance for the book, she styled most of the food and props in the studio photography, and contributed a number of authentic recipes and photographs from her Italian archive. Adrian Garforth MW helped develop ASK Italian's all-Italian wine list and has shared his passion for Italian wine in the book's wine sections.

At ASK Italian, we must give special thanks to CEO Harvey Smyth whose vision and commitment to the Great Ormond Street Hospital Children's Charity has been the driving force behind the book and behind ASK Italian's commitment to serving authentic Italian food in the restaurants. ASK Italian's project manager on the book has been Jane Ahern whose exceptional ability to organize other people has kept the words and images on track as we hurtled towards the deadline. Catherine Salloux has led the relationship with the Great Ormond Street Hospital Children's Charity and been a great support for all of us working on the book. Anna Stanton has contributed valuable design direction for the book. Jane, Catherine and Anna have championed the look and feel of ASK Italian's brand throughout the book's content.

Adapting the restaurant recipes for home use and testing them all in domestic kitchens has been an enormous job and special thanks go to Jeena Rodrigues, who leads our food development, and Faton Vijita for going well beyond the call of duty to accomplish this. Fari, as we call him, also cooked much of the food for the photography sessions. *Bravissimi!*

John Michael O'Sullivan offered design support for the photo shoots and propping, and kindly allowed us to use his photos from trips to Milan. Martyn Rose contributed photos from a visit to the Esposito brothers in Puglia during the olive harvest. Indeed, thanks to all at ASK Italian who have shared their photos from Italian trips. They've helped bring our passion for Italy and its food to life in this book.

Thanks go especially to the book's photographers: Jamie Laing, who ably shot the majority of the book's food in the studio, and Sylvie Tata, who photographed the people in the book as well as some recipes in the restaurants. Carla Capalbo took the photos of the children at Great Ormond Street Hospital and most of the photos of Italy and its foods. Studio photography was at Icetank Studios, London, where thanks are due to Chris Cooke and studio manager, John Rattenbury, and to Karol Gladki, whose expertise was invaluable in helping to cook the food used in the photographs. Many thanks too go to our restaurant teams in Bromley, Spring Street and Spice Quay in London for hosting our in-restaurant photoshoots and to the customers who participated in them.

Continued over...

Top from left: Jeena Rodrigues, Fari Vijita, Jamie Laing, Carla Capalbo, Adrian Garforth, Charlie Craggs
Second: Theo Randall, Catherine Salloux, Anna Stanton, Steve Edge, Jane Ahern
Third: Karol Gladki, Jane Ahern, Josh from GOSH, Harvey Smyth
Bottom: Sylvie Tata, Liz Garcia, Tom West, John Michael O'Sullivan

Steve Edge, of Edge Design, has provided colourful and creative inspiration on the visual side of the book. His team included Liz Garcia, who played an invaluable role in developing, laying out and pulling the book together. Tom West helped design the book's look and feel. Geo Law drew the chapter opener illustrations. Many thanks go to them all.

We are delighted that several of our Italian expert suppliers and friends also contributed their delicious family recipes: *grazie tante* to brothers Giorgio and Gilberto Greci, brothers Luca and Giuseppe Esposito, Marco Gambino, Vito Ivone, Caterina Mancini and to Martyn Rose. Tori Eeles at Liberty Wines and Neil Westley kindly helped facilitate this.

Other invaluable help from ASK Italian team members came from Charlie Craggs for organisational support behind the scenes, at the painting afternoon at Great Ormond Street Hospital, and for sourcing photos from our Italian trips. Thanks also to Gayle Cassinos and Phil Boyd for collating stories from our ASK Italian team members about their favourite dishes on the menu.

Thanks also go to Jo Lake for handling the commercial aspects of the book, to Chris Gasnier for championing our partnership with Great Ormond Street Hospital Children's Charity internally and for sourcing pictures from Italy trips, to Emma Peters for planning the launch of the book with Penguin, and to Spencer Playle for working out the logistics of getting the book into our restaurants.

The ASK Italian Board members, Jane Bon Bernard, Gavin Adair and Stephen Holmes, have long been supportive in their commitment to the partnership with Great Ormond Street Hospital.

The team at Penguin Books has offered welcome support during the making of this book. Many thanks go to Ellie Smith, Sarah Fraser, Ilaria Rovera, Ben Brusey, Emma White, Joel Rickett, Richard Lennon, Graham Sim and to Caroline Pretty, the book's copy editor. Thanks too to the repro house, Altaimage.

At Great Ormond Street Hospital Children's Charity, sincere thanks go to Tim Johnson, Antonia Dalmahoy, Sarah Norris, Simon Kaston and Lottie Wilkins for their help and enthusiasm for this project. And of course we would like to send a special thank you to the celebrity supporters of the hospital who have kindly shared their passion for Italian food with us all, and to the children and their families who got involved in the project.

Finally, thanks to all our ASK Italian teams for their continuing support and enthusiasm for our Italian recipes and for the book project, and to our many loyal customers who we hope will get pleasure from using the book by learning to cook some of these delicious Italian recipes at home, in the knowledge they've contributed to helping children and their families at Great Ormond Street Hospital in London.

Buon appetito!

INDEX

VIKING

Published by the Penguin Group
Penguin Books Ltd, 80 Strand, London WC2R 0RL, England
Penguin Group (USA) Inc., 375 Hudson Street, New York, New York 10014, USA
Penguin Group (Canada), 90 Eglinton Avenue East, Suite 700, Toronto, Ontario, Canada M4P 2Y3
(a division of Pearson Penguin Canada Inc.)
Penguin Ireland, 25 St Stephen's Green, Dublin 2, Ireland (a division of Penguin Books Ltd)
Penguin Group (Australia), 250 Camberwell Road,
Camberwell, Victoria 3124, Australia (a division of Pearson Australia Group Pty Ltd)
Penguin Books India Pvt Ltd, 11 Community Centre,
Panchsheel Park, New Delhi – 110 017, India
Penguin Group (NZ), 67 Apollo Drive, Rosedale, Auckland 0632, New Zealand
(a division of Pearson New Zealand Ltd)
Penguin Books (South Africa) (Pty) Ltd, Block D, Rosebank Office Park,
181 Jan Smuts Avenue, Parktown North, Gauteng 2193, South Africa

Penguin Books Ltd, Registered Offices: 80 Strand, London WC2R 0RL, England

www.penguin.com

First published 2012
001

Great Ormond Street Hospital Children's Charity. Registered charity no. 235825

Set in FS Sammy, Gotham and Univers Condensed
Typeset by Edge Design Ltd
Printed in China

A CIP catalogue record for this book is available from the British Library

ISBN: 978–0–670–92244–4

ALWAYS LEARNING   PEARSON